THE INDUSTRIAL ARCHAEOLOGY *of* DARTMOOR

By the same author
The Industrial Archaeology of the Peak District
The Bude Canal (with Monica Ellis)
The Grand Western Canal

THE INDUSTRIAL ARCHAEOLOGY of DARTMOOR

Helen Harris

Peninsula
Press

1986 Dedication

To the memory of my husband, Desmond Harris, who would have encouraged me in this revision as he did in the original work.

Peninsula Press gratefully acknowledge the assistance given by The Dartmoor National Park Authority during the preparation of the 1992 edition.

Published by Peninsula Press Ltd
P.O. Box 31
Newton Abbot
Devon TQ12 5XH

Telephone (0803) 875875

First published by David & Charles 1968
Second revised impression 1972
Third edition with new material 1986
Fourth edition with further new material and pictures 1992

British Library Cataloguing in Publication Data
available for this title.

ISBN 1 872640 21 4

Printed in Great Britain by
Redwood Press Limited
Melksham, Wiltshire

Contents

Some sites mentioned in the text are on private land where there is no public access. The landowner's permission should be sought by anyone wishing to visit these sites. There is, however, right of access over much of the open moor. Details can be found on the Ordnance Survey Outdoor Leisure Map 28, Dartmoor.

List of Illustrations

PLATES

Frontispiece (opposite) *The River Plym bordering Brisworthy Burrows, where considerable spoil heaps remain from early tinning. First recorded here in 1168, the extraction of tin was virtually the beginning of industry on Dartmoor.*

DIAGRAMS IN TEXT

PART ONE

CHAPTER ONE

The Beguiling Landscape

DARTMOOR, to the casual first-time observer, might appear to be a natural landscape—natural in the sense of being unchanged by the hand of man through the ages of time—or at any rate as natural a landscape as it is possible to find in the rapidly changing land of Britain. Seen from afar, Dartmoor's unique skyline of sweeping hills, sometimes light, sometimes dark against the sky, their crowns of rugged granite tors piling upwards often into cloud, gives the impression of an area aloof and unchanged, save by weathering, since the early days when volcanic activity beneath the earth's crust caused the outpourings of molten granite which gave to Dartmoor the outline we see today.

And still when one gets nearer to the moor itself, even allowing for the roads and stone walls, such obvious evidence of the hand of man, one may travel some way and be forgiven for assuming that at any rate very little human influence has penetrated to this lonely remoteness, where hillside upon hillside shows no sign of habitation, and where the rivers tumble down in their lovely time-carved beds.

And yet, if one stops and explores but a little way, the chances are that some relic of a bygone industry will present itself. A clapper bridge or a gatepost may appear as a monumental reminder of the work which went into the treatment of surface stone and the wide variety of uses to which it was put, centuries ago. The very undulations upon which one comfortably settles for a picnic beside the stream or river of one's choice are as likely as not the spoil left by tinners who scoured this and so many of the valleys in days gone by, changing the whole appearance of the valley floor as they went.

And in the wider scene, in so many parts of the moor, the landscape is scarred with deep gullies, great indentations into the hillsides affecting the actual contour of the land, the record of intense mining activity in the past. The cutting of peat, on small or commercial scale, has made inroads into the ground's surface and left it scored with parallel lines where once the men worked their 'journeys'. Massive grey faces of hewn granite and tumbled man-made clitter, now again left to undisturbed solitude, speak of past quarrying activities of no small importance, while in some places the sad white tips and milky pools of clayworkings, even if abandoned, still persist upon the landscape.

The further one goes the more obvious it becomes that man—industrious man—has been here before, a fact which becomes tangible should one come across the tracks of some long-disused tramway, perhaps treading on rails of unique antiquity. Not all the streams encountered may prove to be natural watercourses; one which contours a hillside is far more likely to be a leat cut either for man's immediate needs or for industrial purposes. Following such a leat may bring one to an abandoned mine; or it may lead to a disused mill, one of the many which flourished on the borders, to process corn or wool, or for other purposes; or by chance to a group of mills in the very heart of the moor, where ruined buildings and stacks are relics of such a surprising find as a gunpowder factory.

Agriculture, at various stages of history, has left its own marks on the land of the moor. Looked at against the low evening sun, or on a day when a covering of snow is in the last stages of disappearance, lines of cultivation may be clearly distinguished, where farmers of a past age laboured with their ploughs. And this is not to mention the stone walls thrown up by the agricultural 'improvers' of later years.

Dartmoor has in fact acquired its own peculiarly fascinating wealth of industrial archaeology. It differs from that of most other regions, Britain's present industrial centres, where it records the earlier activities of enterprises which generally still continue to flourish on a modern and expanded plane. Whereas in these areas the relics of the industrial past are threatened or destroyed mainly by the industrial present, by thrusting modernization and rebuilding programmes, on Dartmoor almost all industries are quietly abandoned; their obliteration is due to the forces of nature—the ravages of weathering in all its forms and the encroachment of plant growth—more often than to the hand of man; it is also due, of course, to the passing of the generations who can recall the later days of Dartmoor's industries, people whose memories and vivid descriptions can bring to life many of the now derelict scenes. The information which some of these people who are still with us can give is invaluable to a student of industrial archaeology.

Leaving aside the early agricultural activities of moor dwellers, industry on Dartmoor really began with the discovery of tin, with which the region was so richly endowed. Its continued recovery over a period of more than seven centuries inevitably dominates any account of Dartmoor's industrial history. Its existence, and that of other minerals, on Dartmoor is the result of igneous upheaval which occurred millions of years ago. Formerly covered by rocks which formed a mountain system, the molten granite from below forced its way upwards into the overlying strata, forming an enormous hump; gradually it cooled under pressure, and as it did so hardened and crystallized. During the course of time the overlying rocks have broken away and been removed by weathering, leaving the granite exposed. While this volcanic activity was taking place vapours of certain minerals in the granite permeated its cracks and those of the metamorphic aureole—the name given to the overlying rocks which were baked and changed by the great heat—and condensed to form the metallic lodes of tin, copper and other elements.

During the seven or eight centuries in which tin is known to have been worked the periods of chief activity occur in three main phases: the first was in early medieval times, when working was on a primitive scale; the second was around Elizabethan days, when more efficient techniques had developed; and the third and last phase continued through the Victorian era and into the present century, when working was mainly on the left-overs of the former mines. During much of the intervening spells mining continued, but on a reduced scale.

It is in the south-west of Dartmoor that tin first appears in known records, in the middle of the twelfth century; there is no firm evidence that it was worked here earlier. In 1168 it was worked at Sheepstor and near the Plym at Brisworthy,[1] but it is not known under what circumstances, nor by whom it was first found. Dartmoor in those days was an area of extremely low population in the midst of a county which, even taken as a whole, was sparsely inhabited compared with a number of other English counties. But the discovery of tin soon brought other prospectors to the scene, new deposits were found, and before long it was being worked in an increasing number of places on the moor in what must have been a veritable bonanza. For about half a century Devon was Europe's largest source of tin, and for a few people great prosperity was derived from it in those years.

'Streaming' was the word applied to the method used by these early tinners, although the word is also used, perhaps more correctly, to describe a process of a later date. As described in Chapter Two, the tinners worked their way up the valleys of the rivers and streams recovering the heavy black stones and sand containing the ore, which were derived from the parent lodes as yet untapped. Smelting, in the early days, was merely a matter of heating the black stones in a rough hole in the ground, a second and more refined smelting being done at an authorized market town. Later, the introduction of blowing-houses, probably in about 1300, enabled a more efficient process to be achieved.

The tinners became a highly organized body, customary law securing for them certain privileges. Although a landlord could be entitled to a toll for tin recovered on his land, it was not his property, and anyone could work for tin wherever it was likely to be. Dues had to be paid to the Crown, however, and so the 'stannary towns' were appointed, Tavistock, Ashburton and Chagford, and later Plympton, to which the tin had to be taken to be weighed, 'coigned' and stamped, and the dues paid for it. The tinners, fiercely independent and conscious of the rights they enjoyed, had their own laws and a parliament

[1]Pipe Roll 1168. Pipe Roll Society xii p.138.

Page 17   (above) *Interior of left-bank blowing-house at Black Tor Falls, River Meavy, showing doorway;* (below) *A mortar stone in the ruins of the right-bank blowing-house at Black Tor Falls (as they appeared in 1967).*

Page 18 (left) *Downing's House, a tinners' cache situated in a small valley on the right bank of the River Erme, upstream from Piles Copse. Despite some deterioration since this photograph was taken in 1937, the cache is mainly intact. It is locally known as 'Smuggler's Hole'; (right) The row of grooved granite posts at Eylesbarrow that supported the mine's flat-rod power system*

which met on Crockern Tor. Often privileges were abused and disorder resulted from disputes with the King's bailiffs; and unfortunate victims were thrown into Lydford Castle, built in 1195 as the stannary prison.

After the first rush, when immediate supplies of tin ore seemed to be becoming exhausted, the activity showed a decline during the thirteenth century. There was a further setback during the fourteenth century in the form of the Black Death, which affected even this isolated region and caused considerable depopulation. In the year 1355 no tin was produced on Dartmoor at all.

Gradually tin-working was resumed and in the fifteenth century output started to increase once more. New finds were made and the production was considerably stepped up, probably due to the introduction of a primitive form of shaft-mining which enabled the rich underground lodes to be reached. The last few years of the fifteenth century and those of the early sixteenth century were truly the heyday of the Dartmoor tinning industry, which reached its peak production of 252 tons in the year 1524. The building or enlarging of a number of Dartmoor churches in the fifteenth and early sixteenth centuries, notably Widecombe Church, bears witness to the prosperity enjoyed around those times.

Production of tin declined again considerably towards the end of the sixteenth century, stopped altogether during the Civil War, but started again with a small output at the end of the seventeenth century. After a slight improvement for a short while during the early 1700s work came almost to a complete standstill. Life was extremely tough for the tin-workers of those days; many lived in great poverty and life's dangers magnified with the development of the deeper mines.

Towards the end of the eighteenth century interest in tin-mining was revived again and other prospectors came and re-established mines, often on the sites of workings of the earlier days. This was intensified through the nineteenth century, though becoming surpassed in importance by the mining of copper, while other minerals, too, were being recovered with profit. A large number of men were employed in Dartmoor's mines during Victorian times, many of them coming from parishes off the moor and sleeping near the mines during the week. From the end of the nineteenth century mining activities generally slowed down; some continued into the twentieth century, but work was often on a 'stop-go' basis and by 1914 most had ceased altogether. After the Great War a certain amount of surface prospecting continued in a few places, but this was only of the deposited remains.

From the late 1700s onwards other industrial enterprises developed, making further use of Dartmoor's natural resources. Prompted by the demands of the Napoleonic Wars and increased populations, many hopeful people, imbued with the new sense of industrial awareness and the pioneering spirit of the age, looked to Dartmoor as a source of potential wealth. There was to be a new awakening. Dartmoor the remote, for long the reserve of moor farmers and tinners, could now, it seemed, be penetrated, tamed and exploited. The improved mechanical knowledge reaped from the Industrial Revolution and developing communications would help bring this about. But as often as not, disillusionment was to follow.

A new agriculture, a high-level arable husbandry, was the ideal of the 'improvers' who enclosed acres of land out of the Forest while turning a blind eye to the unsuitability of climate and soil. The quarrying era, while it lasted, was more successful; surface stone had for long been the main building material, and was still used for the cutting of setts for paving the new towns, but now mechanical aids made quarrying a reality. Dartmoor granite became a popular material for building in London and elsewhere. Granite quarries were opened at Haytor, and a tramway constructed in 1820 for conveying the massive blocks to the waterway of the Teign. On the west, quarries in the vicinity of King Tor came into being. Some men believed that there was a fortune to be made out of peat, which from early times had been used as a domestic fuel and in the making of charcoal for heating the furnaces of tinners' blowing-houses. Tramways were constructed and plants set up for the extraction of naphtha and other chemicals from peat, but the pioneers had not reckoned with Dartmoor's high moisture level and considerable drying difficulties.

One of the names connected with this period is that of Sir Thomas Tyrwhitt; his well-intentioned efforts to 'open up' and industrialize the moor were far from completely successful, but have nevertheless left their mark on the Dartmoor of today. Tyrwhitt held the office of Lord Warden of the Stannaries, besides being Member of Parliament for Okehampton and later for Plymouth. He was also a friend of the Prince of Wales, holder of the Duchy of Cornwall lands upon the moor. Tyrwhitt was convinced, as were some of his contemporaries, that this bleak and mainly untamed upland was capable of providing a less spartan living for the dwellers who clung to its surface, and even of serving some economic usefulness in the country as a whole.

He started work in 1785 at Tor Royal, building a house and making a farm out of land taken from the Common of the Forest. Ideas for forestry and quarrying also featured in his plans. The village of Princetown, as well as its grim and dominating prison, is a lasting memorial to Tyrwhitt's ambition. It was his idea that a prison to accommodate the increasing number of prisoners resulting from the Napoleonic War, who were at the time enduring severely overcrowded conditions at Plymouth, would be a useful addition to the moor, with the intention that the prisoners could work in the quarries, on the land and in the making of the roads. A site was carved out of the Duchy lands, with the blessing of the Prince of Wales, and the work, under Tyrwhitt's supervision, commenced in 1806. The installation of the French, and later American, prisoners of war very soon brought trade to this formerly barren spot, and for the first time the locality experienced a certain prosperity. The settlement that grew up was named Princetown in honour of its royal benefactor.

When the wars ended in 1815 the prison emptied. But Tyrwhitt had another idea, the construction of a railway between Princetown and Plymouth to add to the road system that was then developing across the moor. His plan was for the railway to bring up lime and sea-sand for the improvement of the land, timber for building, and coal and other domestic necessities. In returning, the railway was to take down Dartmoor's exportable commodities—granite, peat, mining products and the products of his proposed agricultural policy. The project was carried out and the Plymouth & Dartmoor Railway opened in 1823.

Although the opening of the railway injected some renewed life into Princetown's depleted population and caused some revival in the granite quarries, the railway was never a paying proposition and it must have been a somewhat disappointed Tyrwhitt who died in 1833. The prison stood empty until it was brought into use for convicts, in 1850. The railway continued to operate on a dwindling scale through the middle years of the century, until the upper section was eventually sold. After reconstruction to standard gauge this part was reopened in 1883 as the Princetown Railway, continuing thus until its closure in 1956.

Dartmoor indeed had its share of railways, industrial and otherwise. Its fastness was penetrated by tramways serving the industries of peat and china clay, and the development of passenger services eventually caused encirclement of the moor at its fringes, while a branch line, opened in 1866, put Moretonhampstead on the railway map, at least for nearly a century.

But, contrary to the dreams of Thomas Tyrwhitt and others, it never became a region of economic prosperity. Although playing a role in hill farming, and still supporting the china-clay industry and a small survival of granite quarrying, in the main the moor remains what it has always been, bleak, unreceptive, weatherbeaten, its thin acid soil resisting most attempts at cultivation. With annual rainfalls regularly in the 70 or 80 inch category, and in an occasional year even approaching 100 inches, together with notorious winter snowfalls which block roads for days and sometimes weeks on end, Dartmoor has remained an area to be avoided by anyone seeking an easy—or gracious—living.

One highly important commodity of the Industrial Revolution—

coal—is notably lacking on Dartmoor, which indeed is far remote from any coalfields. This contributed as much as other factors to the moor's failure to become a centre of highly developed industry. Also, it became more economic to import tin and copper from other countries, and men demanded better working conditions than could be got by toiling against the hard rigours of the moor in all its weathers.

Where, by degrees, nearly all of Dartmoor's industries of the past have faded away, and where the miners and mill-workers have left, the walker and holiday-maker have stepped in. For those who love Dartmoor as it is, wild and undeveloped, still offering peace, solitude and adventure, the absence of active industry is not unwelcome. Yet the discovery, perhaps unexpected, of remains of man's past labours in a remote spot, adds an historical dimension to a day's exploring and can, with a little imagination, extend understanding of the lives led by a sturdy and distinctive element in Britain's past.

Page 23   *Far out on the moor, by the Doetor Brook (Lydford), are the remains of Foxhole Mine, worked for tin in the nineteenth century.*

CHAPTER TWO

The Early Tinners

THE recovery of tin is the earliest form of industrial activity which we know of on Dartmoor, though its very first beginnings are lost in the receding ages of time. That prehistoric man knew a little about the metallic potential of the ground under his feet seems certain, though the evidence is sparse. The presence of tin ore in the form of a cassiterite pebble and grain of tin slag found in hut remains examined by archaeologists near the River Avon on Dean Moor a few years ago, and now to be seen in the Exeter Museum, is likely to have been an accidental byproduct of iron-smelting which was certainly carried out on Dartmoor in prehistoric times. There is no evidence that any tin-smelting took place there before the coming of the Normans.

When, however, tin-working did properly begin, in the second half of the twelfth century, it quickly became established, and for half a century Dartmoor's production outstripped not only that of Cornwall, but also that of any country in Europe.

EARLY METHODS OF WORKING

The exact methods used by those early tinners as they worked up the valleys of the moorland streams and rivers remain obscure; of necessity they were primitive and crude. In these valleys was to be found the coarse sand and gravel, heavy and black, which was in fact tinstone or cassiterite (oxide of tin) brought down by weathering from the actual lodes. Being heavy, this 'stream' tin came to rest beneath the lighter alluvial material of the valley floor, which the tinners turned over in order to retrieve the ore. Nearer the parent lodes the pieces of cassiterite became larger, and were known as 'shode stones'. With their wooden pans or buckets and shovels the tinners separated the precious tinstone from the rubble waste which they threw up in heaps along the banks as they went. These developed in places into sizeable mounds, and over the years have become covered with lichen and grass, heather and whortleberries. The hummocks are numerous upon the moor, to be found along almost every stream and river valley and forming the chief visible evidence of the activities of the earliest tinners.

The next development in the search for tin was at a higher ground level and involved working on the backs of the actual lodes. Indentations were made into the hillsides as the tin-bearing material was removed with picks. The process was assisted by the action of strong streams of water, artificially diverted to the working area, which by their action swept away the lighter, unwanted waste. Natural springs of water higher up the hillside were of course desirable for this, but where these did not exist a system of rainwater collection was devised. A small reservoir often in the form of a pear-shaped or crescent-shaped pond was dug out, and channels provided to feed in rainwater from the area of the hill above; then further channels or leats were made from the pond to the working area. Remains of these systems can often be seen above old hill-workings, and particularly good examples are described by Hermon French and Mrs D. Linehan in an appendix to a paper delivered to the Devonshire Association in 1963, 'Abandoned Medieval Sites in Widecombe-in-the-Moor'. These are the leats on the south side of Hookney Tor, in North Bovey parish (SX 699811), where a number of different levels lead into the old Headland gullies from Grim's Lake; a pear-shaped pond on Hameldon (Widecombe), north of Stoneslade Tor, at the head of a gully (SX 711785); and a crescent-shaped pond above a large excavation in Manaton parish, on Challacombe Down (SX 691802). Not only the bigger workings were provided with leats, even small individual sites having their streaming channels. Often these old systems have become broken away, during the passing of time, and overgrown with herbage, so that they are not easily definable, although aerial photography can often pick out unexpected features.

All the tin-workings of early days were 'open-air' ones, either in pits like quarries or elongated trenches. Later, the processes of 'costeaning' and 'shamelling', which involved digging a series of shallow pits along the lines of the veins or lodes, took the process a stage further towards the evolution of shaft-mining, which did not come until a later date. It is unlikely that true shaft-mining, as we think of it, was practised to any depth during medieval times; what existed prior to 1700 must have been very primitive, scarcely more than deeper open-cast works—the deep open cuttings or gullies so frequently found on Dartmoor today. Only two shafts made by the 'old men'—the term used by later miners for the early tinners—have been found (during later working at Vitifer and at Hooten Wheals, Hexworthy), and these were probably dug no earlier than the eighteenth century. Mines of any great depth could not be constructed and used before suitable mechanical means of 'unwatering' them existed—water always being present in such abundance and at such a high level on Dartmoor.

Life for the early primitive miners was harsh enough. Some idea of what they had to endure was given in the seventeenth century by T. Westcote in *A View of Devonshire*.

> No labourer whatsoever undergoes greater hazard of peril or danger, nor in hard or coarse fare and diet doth equal him: bread, the brownest; cheese, the hardest; drink, the thinnest; yea, commonly the dew of heaven, which he taketh from his shovel, or spade, or in the hollow of his hand. . . . He spends all day (or the major part thereof) like a mole or earthworm underground, mining in deep vaults or pits, as though he intended (with noble Sir Francis Drake) to find a way to the antipodes; yea, a nearer, and so to surpass him: for it is somewhat of that profundity, that notwithstanding the country (so they term the earth over their heads) is propped, posted, crossed, traversed, and supported with divers great beams of timber to keep them in security, yet all is sometimes too little; they perish with the fall thereof notwithstanding.

CRUDE SMELTING

The quantities of 'black' tin obtained had then to be converted to 'white' tin by smelting; in the early days this was a rough-and-ready process. The first method consisted simply of lighting a fire in a depression in the ground, near the source of the ore, placing the metallic pebbles in the fire and later retrieving the tin from the ashes. This was obviously inefficient, and a second, more refined, smelting was necessary when the resultant material was taken to one of the authorized stannary towns. Later the tinners learned to pile the pieces of ore into cones, surrounding these by hard clay; this was heated from a furnace below, worked by bellows, the molten tin discharging at the foot. Furnaces of this type were later made of granite.

THE BLOWING-HOUSE AND ASSOCIATED EQUIPMENT

A real advance in efficiency was the progression to blowing-houses, probably first used in the early fourteenth century. The more efficient smelting process possible in these resulted in a much purer end-product, the white tin retrieved reaching, in fact, an exceptionally high standard of purity. A single smelting in a blowing-house was adequate for standard requirements.[1]

The buildings were constructed of stone and turf, with thatched roofs, and were situated on the banks of streams where the fall of water was enough for a leat to be constructed to work a small overshot waterwheel. A fall in the stream of about 12 ft in a fairly short distance was necessary, though sometimes a longer distance resulted in a leat of quite considerable length. A wooden launder conducted the water from the leat on to the wheel, the diameter of which would be between 8 and 10 ft.

Inside the building would be a stone-built furnace, with a fire of charcoal fanned by bellows activated by the waterwheel. The crushed ore and charcoal, layer upon layer, were laid in the furnace, and during the operation the molten tin would drop through its base into a stone float, from which it was ladled into moulds. From these ingots of white tin were produced, of 200 to 300 lb each.

Before being put into the furnace the ore had to be reduced to a

[1]The term 'tinners' mill' is now preferred by archaeologists to cover both crushing and smelting sites. On many sites the two processes were combined.

sufficiently fine state. This was done by pounding it on a block of hard stone made to serve as a mortar or anvil, using as a pestle perhaps a metalbound piece of wood, or a ball of stone. When the mortar-stone's first concave depressions became too deep for convenient use, the tinners just changed to another part of the stone's surface, or turned it over and used the other side: the evidence of this is the discarded mortar-stones with more than one of these depressions to be seen on the sites of many tinners' mills. Alternatively, the arrangement on many stones of mortar-hollows in fairly regular alignment, two or three holes at a time, suggests that some mechanical means may have been in use, a two or three-point stamp-like device working up and down to crush the ore lying on the mortar-stone. Diameters of the holes in mortar-stones vary, but average around 8 in, though some have been found as broad as 12 in; depth is usually around 4 or 5 in, but can be rather more or less.

At another piece of equipment used in preparing the ore for smelting was the crazing-mill. This consisted of two circular granite millstones, one on top of the other, the upper one being made to rotate on the lower one which was fixed; the ore, already partly prepared, was placed between them, and was subsequently crushed to fine particles. There is no evidence that all the mills were equipped with this particular, more advanced, piece of apparatus, only a few having been found, amongst them a pair near an old blowing-house at Gobbet, on the River Swincombe. The crazing-mill may have been revolved by water power, or perhaps by either man or horse power.

At a later date knacking-mills, or stamps, were regularly in use for reducing the larger pieces of ore to a fine enough state to be dealt with by a crazing-mill; improved stamps in fact eventually obviated any need for the latter. The early stamps consisted of a set of upright pieces of strong heavy timber, their lower ends metalbound, which, by water power, were made to work up and down to crush the dry ore beneath them; it was when the method of crushing the ore wet under the stamps was brought in, near the end of the sixteenth century, that the subsequent use of the crazing-mill could be dispensed with.

Stamps, of a more modern kind, were employed up to the very last days of mining on Dartmoor. Evidence of the existence of a knacking-mill at an early date near the River Erme is indicated in the name of Knacking-Mill Gulf, a small valley on the river's right bank.

The necessity for the knacking-mill, to deal with the larger pieces of ore, really resulted from the increasing depth of the workings: the material brought from the vicinity of the actual lodes was of a lower grade than the stream tin, which was in smaller pieces and of a richer tin content.

THE STANNARY TOWNS

It is improbable that the mining and treatment of the ore were carried out simultaneously. More likely, mining would continue for a spell until ore had accumulated, and then the tinners' attentions would be turned to crushing and smelting. This would normally be done twice or four times a year, to precede the periods of coinage at the four stannary towns. The appointment of Tavistock, Ashburton and Chagford as official centres for the marketing of Devon's tin dated from 1305. In 1328, after a successful petitioning on the grounds of better export facilities, Plympton was appointed a stannary town in place of Tavistock, but due to its subsequent protests Tavistock was allowed to continue as a centre, and Plympton became a fourth one.

At the times of coinage the controller and receiver visited the towns, complete with stamping-hammer and weights which were carried in a sealed bag, and there followed a busy few days. The tinners sent in the metal they had to sell, usually by pack-horse, and, as well as stannary officials, the presence of intending purchasers, dealers in tin from other parts of England besides a few Flemish and Italian traders, and pewter factors, helped to fill the town. With due ceremony and formality the tin was stamped with the owner's name, weighed, 'coigned' (the corner taken off with hammer and chisel by the assay master) and valued. Then coinage dues were paid out.

Tin in those early days was largely required for the making of pewter, the principal material used for plates and mugs. London was the main pewter-manufacturing centre in this country and to there the heavy blocks of tin were shipped. The easiest and most direct routes for laden pack-horses going from the stannary towns to the sea can be surmised. From Tavistock tin was probably carried to the quays at Morwellham, on the Tamar, or it may have travelled further overland direct to Plymouth. Certainly tin received at Plympton would have been exported via the Plym—a river which was feeling the effects of the tinning industry in other ways, judging by the continual complaints of silting in the estuary caused by operations on the moor. From Ashburton shipment may also have been made from Plymouth—or perhaps from the Dart at Totnes or Dartmouth; while tin from Chagford must have found its way to the Exeter waterside.

LEVELS OF PRODUCTION

Fairly accurate records exist for four centuries of the tinning years —mainly due to the stannary system and its interest to the Crown. The following table shows the total production of white tin on Dartmoor over periods of fifty years, as well as the average annual productions within those periods.

	Tons	Average tons per year
1400–50	2,704	54
1450–1500	5,196	104
1500–50	9,944	199
1550–1600	4,655	93
1600–50	1,250	25

Highest production in any year recorded was 252 tons in 1524; the tin industry on Dartmoor was indeed in its heyday during the first half of the sixteenth century. It is interesting and surprising, however, to note that this figure was probably exceeded by the production of the very early years, for it is estimated that between 1171 and 1189, when all the virgin stream deposits of tin were being exploited, average annual production reached 343 tons. In the following (thirteenth) century there was a considerable drop in production, and records are incomplete, though it is known that for the closing years of the century the annual average was around 33 tons.

EXISTING REMAINS OF TINNERS' MILLS

The remains of a number of the old tinners' mills—often known in bygone days, for some reason which is not completely clear, as 'Jews' Houses'—still exist today and can be found at various places on Dartmoor. The word 'remains' however must be emphasized, as all those that can still be identified as such are in ruins; nevertheless certain characteristics can be clearly seen in many of them. The greater number of these lie mainly near the rivers and tributaries in the southern part of the moor, the northern section with the banks of the northward-flowing rivers showing little or no such evidence. R. Hansford Worth, whose painstaking study and surveys contained in a number of papers presented to the Devonshire Association are of such value to those interested in the moor, has included in his observations a study of blowing house remains, and in his book *Dartmoor* has listed over forty sites. Finds in recent years have increased the number of known sites of tinners' mills to over a hundred, mostly dating from around 1450–1650, with over sixty of the sites retaining structural remains. They have been listed by Dr Tom Greeves in an article in *Dartmoor Magazine 23* (Summer 1991), in which he also states that only fifteen sites are of definite 'blowing' mills, most having been used for 'knocking' (or 'knacking')—the process of crushing ore or slag.

The following are descriptions of a selected few typical and reasonably well-preserved examples, displaying different features, in different parts of the moor, which can be reached without too much difficulty of approach.

At Black Tor Falls, River Meavy (SX 575716)

The remains of two tinners' mills exist here, one on each bank of the small river. They can conveniently be reached from the Yelverton–Princetown road across Walkhampton Common (B 3212) near Black Tor. A walk past the tor and down the slope on its eastern side to the river below will bring the waterfalls into view and the remains of the buildings just below them can be seen.

The building on the left bank consists of two sections, a larger section with an area of about 17 ft × 15 ft, and a second, smaller, one adjoining (plate, p. 17). The most outstanding feature is the doorway, with its lintel still in position. On the outside of the lintel are the Roman numerals XIII, but the significance of this is not known. Power probably came direct from the stream, with no leat, but remains of the underground tail-race can be seen.

The right-bank building must have been rather smaller. The remains of a fireplace, partly collapsed, can be clearly seen, and the route of the leat can be traced. Some discarded mortar-stones can be found, lying amongst the fallen stones inside and outside the building. Just south-west of the building are apparent dressing-floor remains.

Beside the River Walkham, above Merrivale Bridge

There are the remains of two tinners' mills on the east bank of the Walkham upstream from Merrivale Bridge on the Tavistock–Princetown road (B 3357). The first, at SX 553753, is fairly large, about 32 ft × 15 ft 6 in. The furnace is reasonably well preserved and beneath it is a float. There is also a mould-stone, with a sample mould in its rim. The second building, about half a mile farther upstream, is of approximately the same area. There are remains of a wheelpit and a mould stone.

On the west bank, at SX 551766, are the very interesting remains of a further, composite tinners' mill, currently being archaeologically excavated by the Dartmoor Tinworking Research Group. It includes a fine mould-stone, with sample mould in its rim (plate, p. 34).

At Week Ford, by the West Dart (SX 663723)

The mills here can be reached by leaving the Hexworthy–Holne road at Saddle Bridge, crossing the stile and following the path down the right bank of the O Brook to its confluence with the West Dart. The stream at its foot can be crossed by a footbridge and the mill ruins easily reached. The ruined buildings are not hard to find, they lie a short distance up the hillside on the O Brook's left bank. A number of mountain ash trees grow nearby.

The higher of the two buildings has a width of about 13 ft, and the longer of the lengthway walls measures around 20 ft. The remains of the furnace can be seen, and, most striking, the wheel-pit, with the track of the leat and the stone base for the launder. Some mortar-stones lie around.

A short distance further down the hill are the remains of another, rather larger, tinners' mill. The position of the doorway is apparent, with a grooved stone jamb. Power here was apparently obtained from the water after it had served the higher building. A mould-stone is to be seen, and a number of mortars.

The exact age of the various tinners' mill remains can only be guessed. The most recent must certainly be over 200 years old, and probably much more, as it is unlikely that any were constructed later than 1740. Some existing then, however, may have been in use to a limited degree up to the eighteenth century. Often blowing-houses were rebuilt on the sites of former ones, for it was the practice from time to time to burn down the building when it became dilapidated (this may well have happened at times by accident as well as design), and in so doing to recover the metallic residue from the fumes which had, during the smelting operations, become entrapped in the thatched roof. In the sixteenth century came the construction of en-larged chimneys, and in these the tin-charged fluedust could be conveniently caught.

In the early eighteenth century reverberatory furnaces came into favour, although the tin smelted in a coal furnace was of an inferior quality to the stream-tin smelted in the blowing-houses, due to the presence of impurities.

A reverberatory furnace with a horizontal flue pipe was in use between about 1822 and 1831 at Eylesbarrow (SX 592676), where, above the valley of the River Plym, the site of extensive tin-workings can be seen (described in Chapter Three, p. 45). The area can be approached on foot along the old track across the moor used by miners, either from a point east of Sheepstor village, where the surfaced road gives way to the track below the northern slopes of Gutter Tor, or alternatively from the opposite direction by picking up the track south and west from near Nun's Cross Farm, which is approached from the road from Princetown to Whiteworks. Eylesbarrow was the last tin-smelting site on the moor, and must represent the transition to the later stage, that of true mining.

Page 34   *Mould stone in the upper Merrivale tinners' mill (west bank of R. Walkham), showing a sample mould on the rim.*

Page 35 (above) *A circular buddle, almost overgrown, near the West Webburn; once used for washing ore;* (below) *A stream of water falls from the arched portal of a wheelpit drainage channel at East Vitifer Mine*

Page 36   (above) *Silverbrook Mine, Ilsington, from a nineteenth-century drawing by Frederick Foot in the Torquay Natural History Museum;* (below) *The engine house of Wheal Betsy on Black Down, Mary Tavy*

CHAPTER THREE

Later Mining

AFTER the medieval tinners' period of relatively high-level activity on Dartmoor and the boom years of the early sixteenth century, quieter times settled over the moor, and tin mining took a role of lesser importance. In the middle of the seventeenth century, at the time of the Civil War, it ceased altogether, and although restarted later, production was small and improved only slightly at the beginning of the eighteenth century before coming almost to a full stop once more. With water still the enemy, operations in these years remained confined to relatively shallow surface workings, usually in the form of cuttings into a hillside; the only two shafts discovered (at Vitifer and at Hexworthy) were shallow by mining standards.

Towards the end of the eighteenth century, encouraged by the Industrial Revolution's technical developments and by the resultant keen demand for metals, back came prospectors and speculators to probe the moor's resources. This later mining period intensified during the mid-nineteenth century, decreasing towards its end and surviving in only a few places into the early twentieth century. Often it was on the sites of the workings of the 'old men' (who had skimmed the cream off the tin lodes) that new prospects were made, but where it was thought it would be profitable to mine at greater depth the newly-learned techniques were put into effect and more capable mining gear went into action. Not only was it on the high granite part of the moorland area that mining was in progress at this time, but all around the borders old workings were being reinvestigated and new ones opened up.

But levels of tin production were low compared with those in medieval times, and were not continuous, the working of mines being sporadic, depending on fluctuating prices governed by the national demand. New prospects were often made with excessive optimism;

37

they might be productive for a time but would soon be worked out; or, sometimes, the mine became flooded. The best and most easily recoverable tin had already been removed, and with the availability of cheaper tin from Malaya such workings became uneconomic.

The peripheral region, the metamorphic aureole, consisting of different rocks—shales, sandstones and limestone amongst them—which had been altered by heat at the time of the granite's upheaval, was proving in places to be a rich source of minerals other than tin, capable of yielding quantities of lead, silver and zinc, copper and arsenic, as well as iron and other commodities in various forms. The yields of tin thus receded in quantity and became of much less importance than those of copper, which took pride of place during the nineteenth century; the copper mines on the edges of Dartmoor shared in the prosperity of the other important ones in west Devon and across the Tamar in Cornwall. Between them all they were in the 1850s producing over half the copper used throughout the world.

The number of mines known to have existed on Dartmoor and its immediate boundary since the end of the eighteenth century is between 100 and 120, the figure depending on whether a number of small prospects carried out mainly as trials are included, and upon where the boundary is drawn. Of this number only about a quarter of the tin and iron mines were in the granite area, the remainder being in or just outside the metamorphic aureole, indicating the importance which this part of the Dartmoor country took on. Often there are records of tin and copper, and other minerals too, being obtained from the same mines. The presence of the different metals occurs fairly generally at points in the border area, and they are not confined to separate clearly defined sections. One cannot travel very far anywhere along the edge of the granite without being in fairly close proximity to mining remains of some sort.

For these more modern miners to win the tin that had escaped their predecessors, and to obtain the other desirable metals, it was generally necessary to use the new means becoming available to penetrate beneath the earth's surface. Not that Dartmoor's natural geography

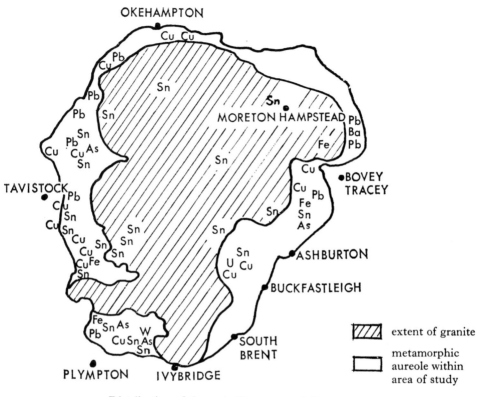

Distribution of the main Dartmoor mining areas
Sn, tin; Cu, copper; Pb, lead; Fe, iron; As, arsenic;
W, wolfram; Ba, barytes; U, uranium)

was entirely hostile when it came to mining; water in superabundance
there might be, but the undulating character of the moor was to an
extent an advantage in gaining access to the underground lodes, and
could also be exploited in the removal of the water. By cutting tunnels
at different levels into a hillside the lode could often be reached almost horizontally instead of by a vertical shaft, and water could be
drained away from the area of working, where this was not below
valley level, without the necessity for pumping. These tunnels or

channels, the 'adits', provided a cheap and simple method of un-watering, used as they frequently were in conjunction with shaft-mining. But, of course, where shafts went deeper than valley-floor level, and where no convenient valley or hillside was available, some method of lifting the water had to be devised. Here again nature was turned to advantage where possible, water being channelled into leats so that waterwheels could work the machinery. Indeed, there were many mines which never relied on anything more elaborate than water power, a cheap and efficient method and a considerable im-provement on hand-operated windlasses or primitive pumps, or whims powered by horses.

In the nineteenth century, however, still better means had of course become available. Watt having applied his steam engine to the Cornish mines, more effective pumping machinery had been de-veloped. The lifting of the ore and waste from the mines could now be mechanically assisted, and on the surface, trucks running on rails, pushed by men or pulled by horses, had become commonplace. Im-proved methods were evolved for dressing the ore, which was now sent away 'black' or unsmelted. Explosives—gunpowder and later dynamite—came into general use to supplement the miners' picks in obtaining the ore.

In sinking the shafts and in making drivages from them mining engineers could draw on a widening knowledge of geology. A number of the Dartmoor mineshafts were constructed on an incline following the lode down its dip (often, in the way described previously, from a hillside) on what is known as the 'drift' principle. An adit would provide drainage, where feasible, from the bottom of the mineshaft, and where this was extended below adit level, pumping would be necessary. It became the practice to work the back of the lode by 'stoping' from the shaft. This involved cutting into the lode in a series of upward steps, one man working behind another, and often these were continued until they worked out at the surface, perhaps intersecting some old surface workings. Where the lodes were rich there might be layers of these stopes, and the shaft would be deepened, and levels cut from which further stoping could be done. Shaft depths varied from a few fathoms below ground level to a hundred fathoms or more, the deepest in the area being 220 fathoms at Wheal Friendship, Mary Tavy, reached in 1875 when copper was being produced there. Needless to say, mines of such depth necessitated a considerable quantity of mechanical gear for unwatering and working.

Extensive information about the Dartmoor mines is given by H. G. Dines in Volume II of *The Metalliferous Mining Region of South-West England* (1956), where the extent and directions of the underground workings are described, with other particulars. Based largely on the plans deposited in the Mining Records Office in London, the details are inevitably incomplete, since many mines kept no record at all of their underground workings, extensive though they might have been, and the plans of others were not always kept up to date during working: and when the mine closed interest was lost.

What is left now of these Dartmoor mines? At the surface the site of an old mine is nearly always marked by undulations, often considerable, due to collapsed underground or surface workings and to spoil heaps, though often these have become partly obliterated by vegetation. It is in fact almost impossible to comprehend the extensive and intricate underground systems described by Dines in relation to a particular mine, and to picture in action the leats, launders and waterwheels, buildings, mechanical apparatus and perhaps tramways, accompanied by the seething activity of tough, toiling men and sometimes women too. But sometimes an open or filled-in shaft can be seen, or the course of a leat and maybe a wheel-pit; some shafts and adits can still be entered (usually only by wading in deep water), though this is a specialized form of exploration only to be undertaken by those with the necessary equipment and experience; occasionally walls of buildings remain, perhaps indicating where the ore was treated; and a few old chimney stacks still stand. At Wheal Betsy, near Mary Tavy, a substantial part of the fine old engine-house still exists, restored by the National Trust in 1991.

Two points should, however, be borne in mind before considering

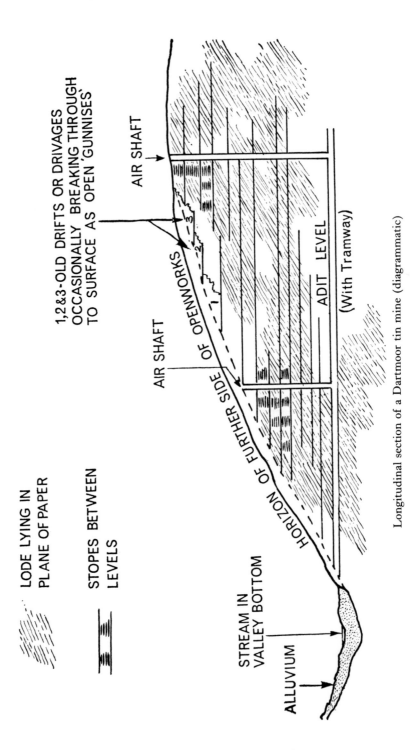

Longitudinal section of a Dartmoor tin mine (diagrammatic)

LODE LYING IN PLANE OF PAPER

STOPES BETWEEN LEVELS

1,2&3-OLD DRIFTS OR DRIVAGES OCCASIONALLY BREAKING THROUGH TO SURFACE AS OPEN 'GUNNISES'

AIR SHAFT

AIR SHAFT

OF OPENWORKS

HORIZON OF FURTHER SIDE

ADIT LEVEL

(With Tramway)

STREAM IN VALLEY BOTTOM

ALLUVIUM

the exploring of old mining remains. One is that they should never be approached without caution. Many people do not realize that in areas like that at Vitifer, where surface working is much in evidence, a great deal also exists underground; what may appear to be the bottom of a shallow pit in a gully may in fact be the top of a choked mineshaft plunging perhaps hundreds of feet straight down; the 'floor' is sometimes only a few feet thick consisting of boulders and gravel jammed against rotting timber. And even the lesser hazards to be found around old workings can, when partly obscured with plant growth, be easily fallen over or into with unpleasant results. The other point is that many old mines, particularly those in the area of the metamorphic aureole, are in private grounds, and the owner's permission should be sought before any investigations are made.

Confusion sometimes arises when examining records of old mines due to the variations in their names. 'Wheal', an old Devon and Cornish word for a mine, is often the prefix to a Christian name or some other, often picturesque, word: for example Wheal Emma, Wheal Mary Hutchings, Wheal Jewell and Wheal Friendship. In addition some mines, perhaps at different stages of working, may have been known by different names, which often refer to their situation; Wheal Emma, for instance, was more latterly known as Brookwood Mine. A number of mines may at a later stage have been worked together and were then known under a collective title, as in the complicated instance in Ashburton parish, where a number of different 'Wheals' were combined as Ashburton United, besides being known generally as Owlacombe Mines from the place where they were situated.

TIN

Tin production on Dartmoor in the period from the mid-eighteenth century onwards showed some revival compared with the immediately preceding years, due partly to the demands caused by the Napoleonic Wars and also to the recently evolved process of plating iron with tin, and the development in South Wales of tinplate manufacture for supplying the varied needs of the new industrial age. But, as already said, the level of production was nowhere near that reached in the time of the earlier tinners. Those who came in these later days were doing little more than glean the remains which their predecessors had left from the pickings of the previously untapped resources. Smelting of tin on the moor had ceased by the early part of the nineteenth century, and in 1838 an Act was passed abolishing the payment of dues on coinage. The fluctuating market value made the tin-mining industry uncertain and caused intermittent working. Increased imports kept down prices, but when the demand for tin exceeded the supply, mines which had closed would reopen and work again for a spell. The demand caused by the tinplate industry reached a peak in 1870, but after this declined. In the year 1893 the total quantity of tin from all the Devon mines was only 52 tons—this being 'black' unsmelted tin of less than 65 per cent metallic content—a point to remember when comparing nineteenth-century figures with those of medieval times, when quantities given refer to 'white' (smelted) tin.

This tin ore, though unsmelted, was far from being crude as it left the mine, for improved methods of crushing and dressing had been evolved so that it could be sent away in a more refined form. In the nineteenth century hydraulic stamps of greater power and efficiency had been developed. On being brought out from the mines on trolleys, running on rails and usually pushed by the men, the ore was treated by stamping-mills, the vertically working crushers reducing it to an increasingly fine and eventually sandy condition, following which it was washed in large circular troughs known as 'buddles'. These were of 18 to 20 ft in diameter, and in the centre was a raised dome from which rotating brushes or arms with a covering of sacking kept the surface of the deposited material even. In this way the heaviest particles, rich in metal, could be separated, and by washing in a series of buddles a high-grade ore could be obtained. Often low-grade ore rejected in previous years could be submitted to the more efficient process and made productive.

It is still possible to see the sites of stamps and adjoining 'floors' on which the ore was further treated, and the remains of buddles exist at a few places, including Hooten Wheals, Hexworthy, a mine which is later further described. There are also the remains of two overgrown buddles of smaller diameter (about 12 ft) and probably older, in marshy ground beside the West Webburn (SX 686796, plate, p. 35), south-east of Soussons Down forestry plantation.

In some places, such as Owlacombe, the ore, which still contained impurities, was further improved by baking in ovens known as calciners. It remained in these for twenty-four hours, men turning it regularly to prevent clogging, and was put in sacks when chocolate brown in colour. (Arsenic was produced from the smoke from the process—see p. 64.)

About fifty of the Dartmoor mines are known to have produced tin at some time during this period, twenty or so of these in the granite, the remainder in the metamorphic aureole.

Tin-mines in the granite area

For many of the mines in the granite area there are no records of production figures, but in the majority of cases yields were probably small, the largest being Birch Tor and Vitifer, Hexworthy, Whiteworks, and East Vitifer and Great Wheal Eleanor. The main feature of the remains of most of the mines in the true moorland area, especially those not worked since the earlier years of the nineteenth century, is usually the pronounced cuttings and humps in the ground, but some have remains worth seeing.

Eylesbarrow (SX 592676 & 598681) has already been mentioned and its situation described (p. 34) as being the last place on Dartmoor where smelting was done. The ruined walls of the old smelting house, covering an area of 60 ft × 20 ft, can still be seen (SX 592676), and from the northern wall the grass-covered length of the horizontal flue which carried the fumes from the reverberatory furnace is still plainly visible. The house also contained a blast furnace. Also to be seen are the remains of the wheelpit and leat. (This building is obscured from the nearby track by a slight rise of ground. It is on the western side of the general area, is reached from a short length of track branching south off the main one, and lies in a slight depression.) There are also remains of tin-stamping houses stretching down towards the Drizzlecombe valley. The considerable remains on the higher ground are chiefly those of a farmhouse and buildings which were put up between 1823 and 1840. A line of pairs of short, grooved granite posts of varying height on the north side of the track—each pair about 20 ft apart—constitute the supports for a flat rod system by which power was conveyed from a wheelhouse below to shafts farther up the hill, for the purpose of pumping water (plate, p. 18). Amongst the considerable number of undulations and open cuttings, most now thickly clothed in heather, can also be traced some of the leats used to serve the mines.

Whiteworks (SX 612710) lies a little over 2 miles from Princetown, in a south-easterly direction, and about the same distance from Eylesbarrow. This open area, 1,200 ft above sea level, with Foxtor Mires stretching away to the south, is of course deserted now and usually peaceful, in sharp contrast to what it must have been a century ago. Clefts in the hillside, unnatural undulations and the remains of shafts, tumbled pieces of walling and vestiges of dwellings all speak of a busy mining scene. The mine was being worked during the nineteenth century at various dates; it is known to have been in action in 1820, though closed in 1826, and working again in the 1860s. In 1870 it was producing a little tin and between then and 1876 produced 96 tons. There were three shafts at this mine, the man responsible for its later working being Mr Moses Bawden of Tavistock, whose name was well known in mining circles at that time. Work seems to have ceased soon after the last records, though the stamps, waterwheel and launder were still remaining in 1890. Subsidence in 1942 caused further obliteration of some of the old workings.

By far the most important and extensive group of tin-mining remains on Dartmoor is around Birch Tor and Vitifer (SX 680810 etc);

part of the area is 1,400 ft above sea level, and it includes a group of mines lying on the borders of Chagford, Lydford, North Bovey and Manaton parishes. It is situated mainly to the east of the Two Bridges to Moretonhampstead road (B3212) close to the Warren House Inn. Birch Tor and Vitifer are the chief mines and the main scene of past activity, but in the near vicinity are also Golden Dagger (SX 682803; see p. 207), East Vitifer (SX 708823; see p. 210) and a number of smaller ones—Headland (SX 694811; see p. 210), Bushdown (SX 680818), King's Oven and Water Hill (SX 675812) and West Vitifer (SX 679828; see p. 191).

Mining here was on the site of much earlier tinning activity, the valley of the West Webburn, like so many others, having been 'streamed' years before. It is known, too, that there was an earlier shaft sunk here: Robert Burnard, addressing the Plymouth Institution in 1891, and referring to Vitifer, recalled that, 'The adventurers found, on opening up the ground early in this century, a shaft, sunk by the "old men" fifteen fathoms deep, which was circular and lined from top to bottom with a stone wall, fairly and neatly put together. This shaft was deepened and worked by the Vitifer Company with great success.'

Quantities of tin were taken from the backs of the lodes, by cuttings into the hillsides, and by shafts, in the late eighteenth century and through the nineteenth. In 1820 Vitifer was working on a large scale, being with Whiteworks and Eylesbarrow the only mines operating on Dartmoor at that time. In the middle years of the nineteenth century over a hundred men were employed, in underground workings, the deepest of which was 70 fathoms, and in the stamping, dressing and dispatching of the ore. Although Golden Dagger continued on and off, in about 1870 Vitifer closed, and remained so for thirty years. But in the early part of the twentieth century interests were again revived, more modern machinery was installed, a new shaft of about 70 fathoms was sunk and about twenty men were employed. Water power for the crushing and dressing machines was brought in by a leat, 7 miles in length over a winding course, from a

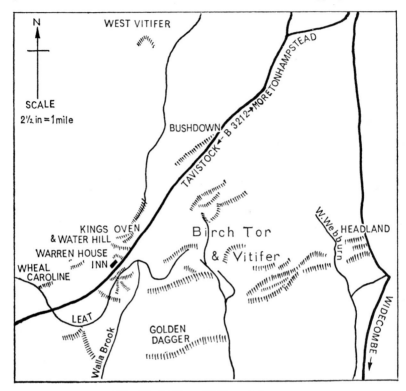

The Birch Tor—Vitifer mining area

point on the East Dart $3\frac{1}{2}$ miles away (p. 205). Working went on more or less continuously until 1914.

Viewing the scene today—the valley floor now overgrown with heather, whortleberries and bracken, with trees of mountain ash and scrub willow, and the water courses meandering and bogging up amongst the spoil heaps—it is hard to picture those important years, in spite of deep gullies which scar the hillside. A few remnants of the stone-built sheds still exist, but no obvious signs remain of the rail tracks along which the ore was brought from the mine entrance, nor of the large wheels—one of them 40 ft in diameter which worked sixteen heads of stamps to crush the ore. Other wheels worked compressors to keep the airways clear, and there were the buddles and other equipment necessary for treating the ore and drying it before its dispatch to the railway then in existence at Princetown.

Men came not only from nearby Postbridge but from places as far afield as Ashburton, Sticklepath and Mary Tavy to work in the mines here; those from a distance would remain for the week, a few lodging in Postbridge, but more of them bringing sufficient food to last until they made their return walk home on the Saturday, 'kipping' meanwhile in a large shed fitted with bunks at the mine itself.

There were also a few cottages in the valley, close to the mine workings, in which some of the employees lived with their families. Headland Warren, where many lived, was a lively place in those days, with the men making their own entertainment after work was over; the Warren House Inn, too, enjoyed a busy trade from the miners. This inn, dating from 1845 and formerly known as Newhouse, replaced a building which once stood on the other side of the road. In out-of-work hours it was a focal point for the community of miners, the centre of countless brawls and celebrations. Conditions of work, though far different from those during the earlier centuries, were extremely tough. In the years preceding 1914 the underground shift was of eight hours' duration, and with the very wet conditions the health of many of the men suffered.

Mostly the mine entrances here were approached horizontally from the side of the hill, the ore being cut out in layers or stopes, one at first, then as the depth increased into the hillside, two or three, the men working at the faces on wood platforms, using picks and later dynamite. Though there are no records of any serious accidents, minor ones, not surprisingly, did occur; a mistimed explosion could catch some workers unawares, and on one occasion a near-disaster was caused by flooding. This was in one of the deepest workings where the men were suspicious that water was threatening them from close behind; shortly after they had come out to the open for 'crib'— their eleven o'clock snack—the water suddenly burst out and flooded the mine. Miraculously the men were all safe, and much of their equipment too, which they had brought out with them, although some of the rails were buckled and trucks damaged.

Not only tin, of which it is recorded that 1,177 tons were sold from Birch Tor and Vitifer in the years between 1854 and 1910, but also iron ore was present in these mines. Latterly this was removed by a magnetic separator, and, being of a type (specular haematite, see p. 68) unsuitable for paint manufacture, was treated as waste, though a quantity was sold in 1926 during a period of spasmodic working in the years between the wars when surface deposits were being worked over. Small quantities of tin ore were sent for a time to South Wales, finally ceasing in 1939.

During the last war most of the metal then still remaining was salvaged and sold as scrap, and besides the inevitable subsidence of many of the workings, new craters were produced by the discharge of unexploded bombs brought here from Plymouth and other places. In 1945 some of the granite from the old stamping-mill which was not already buried under debris was incorporated into Soussons wall close by.

A smaller mining area which also saw commercial activity in fairly recent times was Hexworthy (SX 661711–650713 & 655708). It included mines previously known as Henroost and Hooten Wheals. Again, later mines were sunk on the site of earlier workings, mostly surface ones, though one previous shaft was found here in a gully. Hexworthy mine surrounds the upper course of the O Brook on Holne Moor from its source on Skir Hill to Saddle Bridge, where it passes under the Hexworthy–Holne road before falling to join the West Dart. It can be approached on foot either by ascending the O Brook valley from Saddle Bridge or by following the track which starts near the Forest Inn.

These early workings were reopened in about 1890, though work stopped after a few years—but not before tin of excellent quality had been produced. Operations started again in earnest, however, soon after the turn of the century and continued for some years. A system of leats supplied the water power, though in 1905 considerable

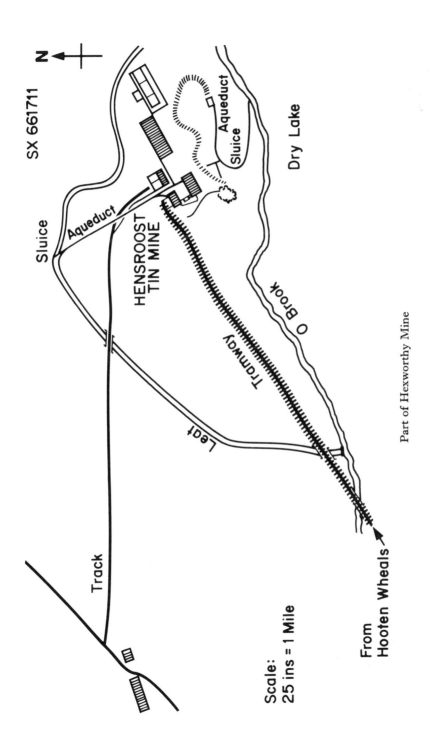

N

SX 661711

Sluice

Aqueduct

HENSROOST
TIN MINE

Aqueduct

Sluice

Dry Lake

O Brook

Tramway

Leat

Track

Scale:
25 ins = 1 Mile

From
Hooten Wheals

Part of Hexworthy Mine

modernization included installation of a Pelton wheel (200 ft head) at Saddle Bridge, about a mile downstream from the mill, to supply electricity. The stamps had coarse grates and the discharge went through classifiers to Wilfley tables, revolving slime tables and buddles, with final dressing in kieve tubs. This last process involved the banging of tubs by relays of men until the concentrate was thoroughly settled in the middle. In this way a fine grade of ore could be obtained, though the practice is now obsolete.

Recorded yields show that in the active years between 1891 and 1909 191 tons of black tin were sold from Hexworthy at a total revenue of £12,493. Thirty men worked here in 1903, coming from such places as Buckfastleigh and Mary Tavy, besides those living at Hexworthy and Whiteworks. Some work continued after the Great War, into the early 1920s.

There are still a good many visible remains of the mining operations at Hexworthy, though American forces practising here during the last war destroyed much that was left. A number of deep gullies and cuttings into the hillside are relics of both later and earlier tinning excavations. A tramway from the vicinity of Hooten Wheals formerly took the ore to an area of treatment works partway down the valley, opposite Dry Lake. Water, taken in from the O Brook at a point just below Hooten Wheals, flowed over a leat and aqueduct to turn the wheel at the Dry Lake works before returning to the O Brook again. There were a number of buildings here, and ruins of some of these still remain, as well as the wheel-pit[1] and part of the raised stone-built embankment which carried the aqueduct. Some ruined buildings beside the track about a ¼ mile to the west provided sleeping accommodation for the men. At Hooten Wheals can be seen the site of stamps used latterly, with the accompanying dressing-floors below on three levels, on the lowest of which are two circular buddles (plate, p. 71). An abandoned armature, lying beside the buddles, bears witness to the electrical power used here. Down at Saddle Bridge, beside the O Brook, are clearly visible the lower parts of the building connected with the use of the Pelton wheel.

[1]This impressive wheel-pit, from which the wheel was removed in 1934–5, was shored up by the Dartmoor National Park Authority in 1980.

Page 53 *The demolition of the mine stack at Wheal Fanny or Crandford, Bridestowe, c 1900*

Page 54 (above) *The former count-house, with its overhanging upper storey, as it remained amid the spoil heaps of Wheal Friendship, Mary Tavy in 1967;* (below) *Ruins of the Wheal Friendship arsenic condensing chambers*

Tin-mines in the area of the metamorphic aureole

Nearly thirty mines in the area of metamorphic aureole are known to have produced tin at some stage since the end of the eighteenth century, the majority of them being in the western and southern border areas. In about half of these tin was produced in company with other minerals, such as copper, and was subsidiary to them. In most the yields were fairly small or not known, but a few mines did produce more than a negligible quantity of tin.

Bottle Hill (SX 564587) lies in Plympton parish, on the hill between the Tory and Smallhanger Brooks. Copper was more important than tin here, though it is recorded that 640 tons of black tin were produced during the middle years of the nineteenth century. There were a number of shafts, but most prominent today is the old chimney stack on the top of the hill which was connected by a flue to calcining ovens in the valley on the east side.

Mary Hutchings and Hemerdon Consols (SX 562580), not far from Bottle Hill, were situated on the slopes of Hemerdon Ball, near the road north from Hemerdon village. Though there is little to see now, they were the centre of considerable activity in the second half of the nineteenth century, a hundred people being employed in 1870, with workings to a depth of 32 fathoms. Tin and arsenic were both produced, the total recorded yield of black tin being 449 tons. Wheal Sidney (SX 550594) was another mine in Plympton parish, east of the road northwards to Shaugh Prior; it had quite considerable underground as well as surface workings, and produced 412 tons of black tin in the years 1854–64 in addition to arsenic. Still to be seen in the area, now afforested, are the remains of workings, tunnels and pits. Two stacks are standing, one in the field, the other in the wood, as well as flues. Parts of the tramway also remain.

South of Yelverton, Yeoland Consols (SX 514663–522663) was worked during the second half of the nineteenth century, when records show 475 tons of black tin were produced. The line of the old shafts and workings of these mines can be traced on Roborough

Down for some distance. Rixhill and Anderton (SX 485723), in Whitchurch parish, were active in the latter part of the nineteenth century when, it is recorded, 529 tons of black tin were produced. Workings formerly extended from near Whitchurch village to the main road (A386) and up the hill further west. Equipment in 1888 included sixteen heads of 'fire stamps' and twelve heads of 'water stamps', but the site was abandoned in 1890. Spoil heaps and remains of some mine buildings and buddles still exist at Anderton Farm and sites of shafts are detectable on the hillside.

Devon United Mines (SX 512786 etc), actually in Peter Tavy parish, being on the east bank of the River Tavy, were rather nearer to the village of Mary Tavy. Consisting of three mines, North, Central and South, they were probably started for copper in about 1820, and on the production of this metal work was concentrated during the early years. Later, however, tin and arsenic were produced, 367 tons of black tin being the output for the years 1904–9 and 1912–22. The workings have been mainly filled with 'tailings' or waste, but numerous dumps, as well as some ruins, and remains of leats, adits and machinery can still be seen.

Owlacombe (SX 770733 etc), in Ashburton parish, covers an area which includes a number of separate ventures latterly brought together under the name of Ashburton United Mines, and worked in conjunction with Stormsdown to the south. The mines were active, mainly in the northern section, during the early part of the nineteenth century, but closed in 1866. In 1906 the mine was taken over by a South African mining engineer who installed new machinery on South African lines. There followed a period of considerable activity, until about 1912, during which up to 200 men were employed, some from as far away as Tavistock, working an eight-hour shift system. The business was not, however, very profitable, and more money was made from arsenic than from tin, of which there was a total recorded production of 348 tons. The mine was later worked for a time after 1930.

Situated between Ashburton and Ilsington, the mining remains lie mainly north-east of Owlacombe Cross south of the Langworthy Brook. Formerly this would have presented an extremely busy scene, with shafts and engine houses, tramlines, buildings and refining equipment, regarded as an important workplace throughout the neighbourhood, with noise, dust and smoke. Today, in contrast, the atmosphere is quiet, nature has largely taken over, and much of the land is wooded. Considerable dumps and various ruined walls still bear witness to the extractive workings of the past. The scene has changed over even the past twenty years. Levelling has been carried out and much demolition, including that of the old 30 ft high chimney stack, built early in the present century. From the chimney, it was said, an Ashburton man working on it in the early days lost his footing and fell from the top to the ground; by a lucky chance, and to the relief of his companions, he picked himself up uninjured, his chief concern being that in the fall he had broken his clay pipe. Much of the building work here was in brick, chiefly white Kingsteignton bricks supplied by Hexter Humpherson, and others marked 'Thomas, Torquay'.

The tramway worked on a system of pulleys and chains and conveyed material from the shafts to the refining areas where there were stamps, dressing floors and buddles, with calciners in which the crushed ore was roasted for the arsenic to be condensed. Power was supplied latterly by electricity generated by a producer-gas engine using coal. Amongst remaining buildings are some of the cottages which formerly housed miners.

Of other smaller tin producers it is worth noting that Furzehill, Horrabridge (see p. 199), produced 196 tons, and Wheal Friendship, Mary Tavy, primarily a copper mine, produced 118 tons of black tin.

COPPER

During the later era of Dartmoor's mining history it was the production of copper which achieved the greatest importance. Though known in ancient times, there is no evidence of any early copper working in this area; but in the nineteenth century, in the days before

the large sources overseas were readily available, the copper production of Devon and Cornwall was of considerable importance. In the
early years of the century more than 40 per cent of the world's
supply of copper came from the two counties, with Cornwall producing the greater part; by the mid-1850s Devon was producing one-
third, and in 1886 over one-half the total quantity, though the years
after 1860, when the climax was reached, saw a rapid general decline.
It must be remembered that only a part of Devon's copper production came from the vicinity of Dartmoor—by far the most important
Devon copper area, Devon Great Consols, lay further west. (See
Frank Booker's *The Industrial Archaeology of the Tamar Valley*.)
Nevertheless, some of the Dartmoor copper mines made a not
inconsiderable contribution to Devon's yields.

There were about forty mines producing copper in the Dartmoor
area, all in the metamorphic aureole or just outside it—none in the
granite. In about half of them the copper existed in the company of
one or more other minerals, usually tin or lead. The sources of
copper were more on the west than the east side of the moor, and remains of mines exist at places from the north-west down through the
Tavistock area to the south-western extremity; the eastern edges of
the moor show few instances, apart from the area of Ashburton and
Buckfastleigh.

The most important of the Dartmoor copper mines was Wheal
Friendship, at Mary Tavy (SX 508794). Covering an area of nearly
thirty acres just east of Mary Tavy village, a good deal is still to be
seen of the remains of the old workings—spoil heaps and partial
walls, wheel-pits, leats and trackways (see also p. 207). What is
visible today of the abandoned mine, however, is little by comparison
with what existed in its active years, to say nothing of the very considerable underground workings. These extended beneath and beyond
the Tavistock–Okehampton road (A386) to the west, and eastwards
to the valley of the Tavy, the deepest workings being to 220 fathoms.

Both copper and lead were raised at Wheal Friendship as early as
1714. In 1796 the mine was reopened by John Taylor, who sunk an

inclined shaft, following the dip of the lode, and production continued under John Taylor & Sons until 1870. In 1838 a recent installation was a large pump worked by a waterwheel, and there was also a
large whim powered by steam. The ore was raised from below ground
by a tramway working on an inclined plane. Throughout the middle
years of the century 150 people were employed at the mine, most of
them living at nearby Mary Tavy and Horndon, and production was
both high and profitable. The ore produced was shipped to South
Wales, transported to Morwellham Quay on the River Tamar by
canal from Tavistock.

The main source of power at Wheal Friendship was water, brought
from the River Tavy by a system of leats. (The Reddaford leat is
described in the Gazetteer, p. 213, and shown on p. 198.) In 1875
seventeen waterwheels were in use, eight of them for pumping, the
largest being 51 ft in diameter with 10-ft breast; four others of rather
smaller diameter operated crushers and stamping-mills. An 80-in
cylinder steam engine stood in reserve for times when water supplies
ran low.

During the 1870s working for copper became unprofitable and the
mine even ran at a loss before being closed down. Work was, however, carried on here after 1880 in the production of arsenic (see later
section), and in dealing with tin ore from this and neighbouring
mines, including Wheal Jewell. This continued until 1925. J. H.
Collins' *Observations on the West of England Mining Region*, 1912,
gives the yields of copper ore for the years 1800–85 as 155,089 tons,
and H. G. Dines quotes the figure of 42,900 tons of $9\frac{1}{4}$ per cent copper
ore for the years 1846–83, 1908 and 1909, while stating these records
to be incomplete.

Nearby, Devon United Mines (already mentioned as producing tin)
also yielded copper ore. Started for copper in about 1820 and worked
at times with Wheal Friendship, in 1846–50 the northerly of the three
mines here (known in the earlier working as East Wheal Friendship)
produced 14,271 tons of copper ore. One or two other less important
mines in the vicinity also yielded small quantities.

In the district immediately south of Tavistock, close to the valleys of the Rivers Walkham and Tavy, amongst a number of other mines, several of which were copper producers, were some yielding quite fair quantities of ore. Wheal Franco (SX 505702), extending along the south bank of the Walkham downstream from Horrabridge village to Bedford Bridge, began working in 1823 and between 1826 and 1862 produced over 10,000 tons of copper ore; in 1838 133 people were employed and the mine was reported to be doing well. The old engine shaft here was 160 fathoms deep and the pumps were worked by water power. In 1857 Franco was one of the most productive of the Devon mines, but in later years a decline set in; water was always a problem and although draining was done in 1870 work never re-started: the demand for copper was waning and many of the miners from this area had already either gone abroad or had left the county to work on railway projects in the home counties or in the new coal mines in the north of England. Signs of leats and shafts can be detected in fields beyond Copperfields residential development.

Another copper producer on this side of the moor was Sortridge Consols (SX 510707), situated between the roads from Horrabridge to Whitchurch and to Sampford Spiney. Main activity was in the middle years of the nineteenth century, when over 7,000 tons of ore were produced (see p. 199). Outside the area, though of some interest, are the remains of Virtuous Lady Mine (SX 474698), close to the confluence of the Tavy and Walkham, reputedly named in honour of Queen Elizabeth I. Work originally started here in 1558 and continued until 1807; in the 1830s the mine was reopened and worked intermittently until being finally closed in the 1870s. The greater quantities of ore were obtained in the later working period, over 4,000 tons being produced in the middle years of the nineteenth century, and in 1870 working was reported to have been to a depth of 20 fathoms, with forty-three people employed—a quarter of the number who worked here in the earlier days. In private grounds, there are considerable remains both above and below ground, and the mine-captain's house is still lived in.

West of Yelverton, copper lodes of the venture known as South Roborough Down (SX 515675 etc) yielded over 1,500 tons of copper ore in the middle 1800s (see p. 191). Still further south is the Bottle Hill Mine near Plympton, already described as a source of tin. It was, however, of greater importance as a copper mine, yielding around 2,000 tons of ore in the early years of the nineteenth century.

Coming around to the southern border region, there were a number of copper mines around Buckfastleigh and Ashburton. Chief of these was Brookwood (SX 718675), situated about 2 miles north-west of Buckfastleigh in the grounds of Brook Manor and, with Wheal Emma, worked during the later years of the century as South Devon United. Around 30,000 tons of copper ore are known to have been raised here during the second half of the nineteenth century. There were six shafts and a number of wheels worked by water from the River Mardle, supplemented by a supply brought from the River Swincombe along a lengthy, tortuous leat constructed in 1859 (see p. 206). Twelve people were employed here in 1870, when the workings were 130 fathoms deep. There are considerable remains—large tips and ruined walls, a sizeable wheel-pit and shafts. One shaft, approached by an adit though open to the sky, still contains the pipe which brought up the water. Nearby are the arched remains of the old engine building.

Not far from Brookwood, close to the River Dart, to the east of Hembury, was the mine known as Queen of the Dart (SX 734688). This was being worked in the early seventeenth century and latterly in the mid-nineteenth, when great hopes accompanied its reopening. A production of 408 tons of copper ore was recorded for 1856. An adit and the remains of a leat have been traced here. There were two shafts, both to the east of the river, and spoil heaps are still obvious, though the ground is now very overgrown.

Other mines around Ashburton and in Ilsington parish also produced some copper, generally with other minerals. Not far away, though over the border in Bovey Tracey parish, was a copper mine at Yarner (SX 783783), worked in the early years and again in the second half of the nineteenth century; 2,300 tons of copper were produced from 1858 to 1865, with workings 50 fathoms deep. Situated now in a nature reserve, there are few visible remains of the mine, though there were formerly two shafts, an engine house and a chimney stack.

The other Dartmoor copper mines of any importance, including the most recently worked, were on the northern fringe of the moor, centred around Belstone and South Tawton. The chief of the Belstone mines was on Greenhill, which can be ascended from the west end of Sticklepath village (SX 632945). The site of two shafts can be seen here as well as a very long ridge-like cupriforous dump—one of the few places on Dartmoor where garnets can be picked up. Another smaller working, Taw River Mine, was on the slopes of Belstone Cleave; probably old, it was reopened in the nineteenth century and was last worked in about 1892. Unwatering was by a 70-ft diameter waterwheel, the pit of which, surrounded by brambles, can still be seen near the road ascending Belstone Cleave, just below Skaigh. In 1892 the mine was considerably flooded and further work ceased, recorded production of copper ore in the years 1867–91 having been 2,934 tons.

Between the roads to Whiddon Down and Throwleigh, close to South Zeal, Ramsley Mine (SX 650930) also included Wheal Emily and was known at different times by different names. It produced substantial quantities of copper. Opened in about 1850, it was worked until about 1880, then after a break had a further spell of activity in the early twentieth century, before ceasing in 1909. At the time of the 1900 reopening a winding engine was installed; this was activated by the unusual procedure of emptying, through a trap-door in the bottom, a tank holding 300–400 gallons of water. In 1902 the mine was producing 100 tons of copper ore a month. It became more mechanized, a steam engine providing the power for raising the tubs of ore to the surface, as well as for driving the pump for unwatering. The ore was conveyed in trolleys by tramway to the crushing and sorting sheds, and down an inclined plane to Drybridge, where it was washed and separated on vibrating tables over which water gently flowed; the mechanism here was water powered. It was really because the very expensive machinery proved not as effective as had been hoped, and because prices fell steeply due to foreign imports, that a general collapse came and the mine eventually closed.

The most prominent relics are the old chimney stack on top of the gorse-covered hill, and the dumps of waste lying around. The metal flue from the steam engine which led to this stack, of the same diameter as its base, before going underground used to run through a large shed, where it provided considerable warmth, and enabled the men coming up from the mine to dry their wet clothes. In the remains of some stonework are recesses which formerly housed the heavy bearings for the engine-room shafting and cable-drum axles. The metal cables, on huge drums in the engine room, ran over pulley wheels on the 'sheer legs' above the shaft and carried the pit cages. The engine shaft, built close to the hillside and now covered with concrete, is obvious from the main road by its stone retaining wall, erected to strengthen its side. The launder which used to cross the Throwleigh road near Drybridge was demolished some years ago, and the old 'floors' by Drybridge were levelled recently as the stonework had become dangerous to children playing there. There is an adit exit, level with the road, in Ramsley hamlet, just north of Drybridge, and another nearby discharges water into the leat. The mine-captain's house still exists, called Owlsfoot, near the main road.

Yields for this mine for the years 1861–80 are given as 6,036 tons of copper, and for 1901–9 as 3,752 tons.

ARSENIC

During the 1860s, when foreign competition was causing the beginnings of a decline in the copper industry in the south-west, attention became drawn to the arsenic often found in association with the copper and tin lodes. Its occurrence in this region is in the form of mispickel—arsenical pyrites, locally called 'mundic'. Earlier in the

century it had been regarded as an inconvenient impurity, and had
been left in dumps around the mines. Later on, material from these
dumps, as well as further ore brought up from the mines, was either
sold in the form of crude mispickel or, in a number of cases, refined
on the spot to produce a purer form of arsenic. As a chemical, arsenic
was in demand for a number of purposes, in the manufacture of
paints, dyes and glass, as a weedkiller and insecticide, and in medicine. Retributively, the formerly despised arsenic often proved more
profitable than the tin or copper.

There are records of arsenic production from at least a dozen
mines on the borders of the moor. In the Mary Tavy area considerable quantities were produced at Wheal Friendship, and smaller
amounts at Devon United and Wheal Jewell (SX 525813). Some
probably incomplete records show that in the years 1846–83 and
1908–9, 17,706 tons of mispickel and 711 tons of refined arsenic were
sold from Wheal Friendship, and in the years 1913–24, in conjunction with Wheal Jewell, 288 tons of mispickel and 1,367 tons of
arsenic were produced. In the vicinity of Plympton the Bottle Hill,
Mary Hutchings and Sidney Mines all yielded quantities of both
mispickel and arsenic, as did others further east, in particular the
mines at Owlacombe, near Ashburton.

In order to obtain the purer arsenic from the ore, the 'mundic'
after being crushed and washed, was roasted in calciners. These were
a series of stone-built ovens from which the vapours passed through
chambers and flues, the arsenical oxide condensing in the form of a
whitish powder. At intervals baffles were opened and men would go
into the chambers and flues to scrape off and collect the arsenical
product. This was dangerous work, arsenic being so poisonous, and
commanded a higher wage. It was necessary for stringent precau-
tions to be taken by the workmen, ears and nostrils being blocked,
mouths padded and hands and feet fully covered, to prevent all possible absorption.

The remains of arsenic-refining apparatus can still be seen. The
best are at Wheal Friendship (plate on p. 54), where there is a metal

flue, and the extensive ruins of the condensing chambers. They are on privately owned ground, however, and access is unfortunately restricted.

These minerals are included in one group as they frequently occur together. Although there has been evidence that one or other of the metals was produced at about twenty mines around the moorland borders, only about nine achieved yields of any note. The most important were those at Mary Tavy—Wheal Betsy, Wheal Friendship (started for lead though later copper-producing) and North Betsy, which yielded zinc. Further north, Kitts and Florence Mines, in Lydford parish, were small ventures, as well as Fanny or Crandford Mine, Bridestowe, which also produced copper (see p. 188).

South of Dartmoor, Boringdon Consols, Plympton and Filham Silver-lead Mine, Ivybridge (really outside the area) both produced fair quantities in the 1850s. In Ilsington parish, Silverbrook Mine yielded lead, silver and zinc, while on the eastern extremity of the Dartmoor border region there were lead mines around Bridford, Christow and Hennock, of which Wheal Exmouth and Frankmills had productions worthy of note (see Gazetteer, p. 193). In this area the mining of barytes has continued until recent times.

Of all these, the remains of Wheal Betsy (SX 510812 etc) are the most spectacular, lying to the east of the Tavistock–Okehampton road (A386) across Blackdown, north of Mary Tavy. The shell of the fine old engine-house with its stack, the last of its kind remaining on the moor proper, has already been mentioned (see plate on p. 36), and surrounding it on the hillside and along the valley of the Cholwell Brook are old workings and spoil tips, dry channels and tracks, and a number of old shafts.

Just when Wheal Betsy was first worked is not known, but it was reopened in 1806 for lead and copper and also produced arsenic and silver. During the following years considerable quantities of lead were raised, some of it being smelted at the mine, yielding about 12 oz of silver to the ton of lead. The rest was dispatched as ore and joined the products of other neighbouring mines in transit over the Tavistock Canal to the River Tamar. During the 1820s, 300–400 tons of lead ore and 4,000 to 5,000 oz of silver were being produced annually. Production continued through the middle years of the nineteenth century, and records for the last nine years of its working give 1,180 tons of 50 per cent lead ore and 2,020 oz of silver. In 1843 the mine was 110 fathoms deep, later to achieve 140 fathoms, and pumping was by water and steam power. Around 1830 fuel for the mine was provided in the form of large quantities of peat brought from the Walkham Head peatworks; but this was not completely successful as difficulty was found in keeping up sufficient heat to maintain a constant pressure, and later coal was used, conveyed via the canal. Wheal Betsy, known also at varying times as Prince Arthur Mine and as North Wheal Friendship, closed in 1877.

Also having interesting remains, on the other side of the moor, is Silverbrook Mine (SX 789759), situated ½ mile from Ilsington village, south of the road approaching the village from the east, close to a stream which flows between woods. It was said to be already 200 years old when working in the mid-nineteenth century (plate, p. 36). Records show that in the years 1854–6 93 tons of 65 per cent lead ore were produced, with 80 oz of silver, and in 1854 and 1857–8, 1,474 tons of zinc ore. Silverbrook employed sixty people in 1857, but was closed by about 1861. Considerable dumps still remain at the mine, as well as the remains of some buildings and a stack.

IRON

Iron has been obtained in quantity in about fifteen places on or around Dartmoor, all being in the east or south, some in the granite and some outside it. The type of ore varies from brown haematite to a variety of specular ore known as micaceous haematite, the sort more often found in the granite.

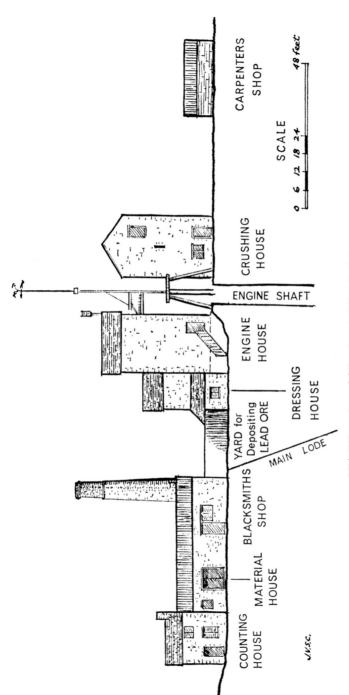

CARPENTERS SHOP

SCALE

0   6   12   18   24   48 feet

CRUSHING HOUSE

ENGINE SHAFT

ENGINE HOUSE

DRESSING HOUSE

YARD for Depositing LEAD ORE

MAIN LODE

BLACKSMITHS SHOP

MATERIAL HOUSE

COUNTING HOUSE

J.V.S.C.

SE/NW section of Silverbrook Mine buildings

The most productive of the iron mines have been in Ilsington parish. The Haytor Iron Mine (SX 772770), worked at first at the surface and later by adit, was in production in the early and middle years of the nineteenth century, and also at times during the early part of the present century up to 1921. An iron ore, magnetite, was found to exist here in company with a variety of other minerals. Local people still remember the ore being brought from the mines to the Bovey road near Blue Burn by an elaborate tramway and carted along the road by traction engines (see p. 200). Nearby Smallacombe (SX 777766) was also worked during the mid-nineteenth century, and produced around 12,000 tons of iron ore in magnetite, brown haematite and other forms. A deep cutting known as the Smallacombe level is all that is left here now. Atlas Mine (SX 778765 and 779762) also produced brown haematite in the 1860s, though in later years it was tin-producing (see p. 200).

Further west, but still in the southern part of the moor, were iron workings at Shaugh on the slopes of the Plym valley (SX 533631; see p. 218), at Boringdon Consols (SX 535577, near Plympton (see p. 217), and at Yennadon (SX 544682 etc) in Meavy parish, where the former surface workings are now marked by undulations.

More centrally, the primarily tin-mining area of Birch Tor and Vitifer was a source also of specular ore, generally regarded as waste, though a small quantity was sold in the later years of working.

Back on the eastern side, Frankmills (already mentioned as a lead producer) yielded some iron ore as well as other minerals, and in the projected area of granite east of the River Bovey micaceous haematite been worked in a number of places. Mostly the working has been by adits into hillsides, usually in comparatively recent years of the present century. The most important site, Great Rock Mine, near Hennock, dates from the 1800s and was worked until 1969.

In the earlier years the ore was used in the iron industry, until the remoteness from the industrial centres and the richer iron beds in the Midlands made it unprofitable. Latterly the micaceous haematite was used for the production of a grey rust-resisting paint.

Ochre and umber, products also derived from iron, have been found in some of the iron mines, and at the Devon & Cornwall Umber Works in the town of Ashburton during the second half of the nineteenth century the product was being obtained from a series of large rectangular pits (see p. 185). Ochre was also sought at about the same time in the parish of Peter Tavy, where remains of the workings can be seen on the western slopes of Smeardon, SX 517782.

WOLFRAM

The tungsten mineral wolfram, used for various purposes including the toughening of steel, has been worked at a mine on Hemerdon Ball in Plympton parish (SX 571582) in recent times, during and immediately following the two world wars. During the 1917–19 period working was opencast, but in the years 1940–4 shafts were also used, and a large mill capable of treating 300 tons a day was installed, though full production was never reached. Recent years have seen a renewal of commercial interest in the working of this particular mine.

URANIUM

Uranium has been found at Kingswood, Buckfastleigh (SX 711666), where earlier trials for copper had been made. Further investigations were made during the 1939–45 war, and have been followed up more recently, but as yet production has not materialized. An adit runs into the hillside.

CHAPTER FOUR

Industries from Granite

THROUGH many centuries the granite of Dartmoor has been taken by man and made to serve his purposes in a wide variety of ways. Its qualities were just as obvious in the prehistoric era as in more recent times, and men of the Bronze Age were quick to make use of its ready availability. Not surprisingly, visible evidence of its use over a long span of time survives all over the moor.

The use of the word 'granite', however, dates from quite modern times, and was almost unknown until geologists came upon the scene; always the rock of which Dartmoor is made was known by the people who lived there and worked it as 'moorstone'. The process of quarrying the granite, too, is of comparatively recent introduction; earlier moor dwellers had no need to quarry, even if such an arduous activity could have been contemplated. There was moorstone in abundance in the form of clitter—boulders and blocks shed from the outcropping tors by weathering over the ages—to supply domestic and other needs, often even without further cutting or dressing. The ancient rights appertaining to the Forest and Commons of Dartmoor permitted the taking of surface stone (though not quarrying) without payment, and farmers who picked the stone off their land to use for other purposes were also making more ground available for grazing and crop-growing.

SURFACE STONE

Undressed surface granite was used by men of the Bronze Age for constructing their hut-dwellings and enclosures, and for their ritualistic monuments and burial chambers, of which many remains are still to be seen. Though the earliest Saxon settlers on Dartmoor apparently ignored stone for building, using instead wattle-and-daub and thatch, later, in medieval times, the cutting and dressing of the

Page 71 (above) *Wheel and stamps at Poldice Mine near Grenofen Bridge in the Walk-ham Valley; photographed c 1887;* (below) *The site of the stamps and dressing-floors at Hooten Wheals, Hexworthy*

Page 72 (left) *Stamping mill at Kit Mine, Colleytown, Sheepstor; photographed 1928;* (right) *Pre-1907 view of Owlacombe Mine, Ashburton, from the north-west*

stone developed and it was put to use for the building of houses and churches, and in the making of clapper bridges for pack-horse traffic. Tinners used the stone close at hand for their blowing-houses, as well as for the equipment to go with them—mortars, furnaces, floats and mould-stones.

There was no difficulty in finding ample stone for the building of walls to enclose agricultural land, while from larger blocks items of domestic and farm equipment could be made. Most of the commons on Dartmoor show evidence of stone cutting from clitter, marks on large blocks showing where they have been cut, and where perhaps a gatepost has been formed. The tors and even prehistoric antiquities were not sacrosanct—many of these suffered and bear marks; the large kistvaen on Longash Common above Merrivale, for example, has on it grooves showing where a farmer cut a gate-post out of it in about 1860; a number of the old granite crosses, too, were made to serve more utilitarian purposes.

All kinds of articles were cut out of the moorstone, right into the nineteenth century; domestic mills (querns), cider and cheese presses and feeding troughs in particular. Belstone Common was one of the places where this was extensively done and where discarded pieces of imperfect efforts can be found, one example there being an abandoned quarter section of a cider press. The village of Sticklepath nearby was probably at one time a centre for the business the industry brought. Close to the right-hand side of the road ascending the hill from Merrivale to Princetown is a circular stone, often mistaken for something of greater antiquity, which is in fact an abandoned apple crusher. Many other such relics are scattered over the moor; long-disused pieces of moorstone equipment lie around on farms, and a number have found their ways to distant gardens of the 'in-country' of Devon to serve ornamental purposes as bird-baths or plant troughs.

In about 1800 the old wedge-and-groove method of splitting stones began to be superseded by the process known as 'feather-and-tare'. A number of holes about 3 in deep, 5 or 6 in apart, were made along the rock to be split, using either a chisel or a metal bar-shaped tool about 4 ft in length called a 'jumper'. In the holes were placed metal wedges called 'tares', these varying from a few inches to a foot or more in length and tapering from an inch or so diameter to a blunt chisel-like tip of about $\frac{1}{2} \times \frac{1}{4}$ in. The tares were supported at the sides by pairs of curved, concave pieces of metal called 'feathers', shaped rather like parts of a bucket handle. They were then repeatedly hit by a sledgehammer until eventually the rock split apart. The presence of half-round holes in a stone is an indication that it was split later than the year 1800. Considerable evidence of such work can be seen soon after one starts to ascend the windblown clitter-strewn slopes of Staple Tor, a short distance north of the road from Tavistock to Princetown (B 3357), just west of Merrivale; many of the granite boulders which lie on the ground display the easily definable line of half-round grooves along a clean break (plate, p. 107).

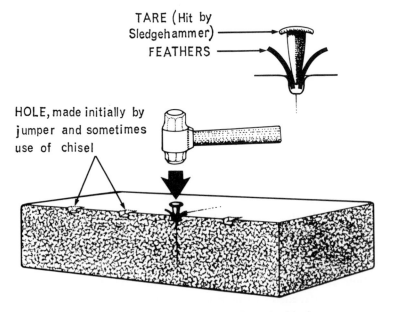

TARE (Hit by Sledgehammer)
FEATHERS
HOLE, made initially by jumper and sometimes use of chisel

'Feather and tare' splitting of granite blocks

For about a century the taking of surface granite and extraction of bedded rock overlapped. An area where surface working proceeded during much of the nineteenth century is that of Pew Tor and Staple Tor on the moor's western side, a few miles east of Tavistock. Freelying granite was available here in conveniently accessible abundance, close to moorland routes that enabled downhill transport to Tavistock—a town currently needing much stone for the developments by the Duke of Bedford, and which, from 1859, was linked by railway to Plymouth, so enabling a wider range of markets. Most of the Pew Tor/Staple Tor area lies in Whitchurch parish, and the smaller part in Sampford Spiney. As the stone-taking moved into commercialism it became the subject of licences granted by the Duchy of Cornwall to various individuals and companies, with arrangements giving consideration to the interests of the respective lords of the manor. Neither Duchy nor manors, however, gained great financial benefits from the leasings, nor even, to any great extent, did the licencees. Reports of illicit taking of stone by those unentitled were constant, as were complaints of depredations and damage to the tors' natural features. Protective lines were defined around the summit of Pew Tor, indicated by specified forms of crosses incised on certain stones. These marks can be seen, as also can much evidence of stone removal—cut-away rocks, and trackways with twin rutted depressions left where carts were run in at lower level for ease of loading. Building ruins beside the Grimstone and Sortridge leat in Beckamoor Combe, at SX 536747, are those of a former smithy, built in about 1871 to serve the trade. The surviving shell was reduced to the present state by destruction in 1964. An old wheel-binding stone lies beside the ruins.

On the southern and eastern slopes of Staple Tor remains of work in the preparing of granite paving stones, kerbs and setts can be found. Amongst the confusion of moorstone clitter still lying around it is possible to discern primitive benches, called 'sett-makers' bankers', made from the natural stone, at which the men knelt or crouched at their labours. Initially it is not easy to pick out these small structures, which were formed by placing two upright pieces of granite about 1 ft 6 in apart into the slope of the hillside, with another slab across the top about a foot above ground level, but the usual occurrence of nearby accumulations of granite chips often provides a clue. Just a few bankers occur on the tor's lower southern aspect (SX 540753), together with some remains of shelter buildings just above. But around to the east, between Merrivale Quarry and the Shillapark enclosures (SX 546755) are many more—twenty or so that are clearly definable and others partly collapsed, positioned either singly or in groups of two, three, or four. One solitary example can even be seen high up against Great Staple's eastern surface clitter. Temporary shelter was often provided over and around the bankers against the rigorous weather that frequently prevails at this exposed altitude of around 1,200 ft.

It was probably from about 1870, for the following five or ten years, that sett-making was in progress on these open slopes. Demand for the products was stimulated by the rapid growth and development of towns at that time, and the need for smooth and solid roads. Most of the Staple Tor setts were taken to Plymouth, and it may well be that much of the granite paving still to be seen in some of the city's narrower streets came from this source.

The larger pieces of granite were broken and cut to a size of 18 in × 9 in, with a thickness of 5 in; these were taken by the sett-makers and cut to smaller sizes. At the bankers the blocks were halved, cut into setts of the required dimensions and dressed with hammers. Payment was by the number of setts cut—one (old) penny per sett, and it was an extremely good worker who could cut sixty a day in order to earn five shillings. Generally around forty would be average. After the establishment of Merrivale Quarry the work was continued within its area, on a bigger scale, until the introduction of tarmac roads eventually destroyed this particular trade. The good qualities of granite for use in pavements are still recognised, however, and some authorities today prefer to relay and retain old granite paving stones rather than replace them with concrete.

Another place on Dartmoor where granite was extracted for the paving of a town was at Yeo, Chagford. In the 1890s Exeter Corporation used granite from fields there for cutting kerbs and channels for the city's Fore Street.

QUARRIED GRANITE

The quarrying of Dartmoor granite started to develop from about 1780 onwards, when the roads across the moor were being constructed and the foundations of Princetown were laid. By 1820 large quantities were being sent away for use in London and elsewhere. But although the demand continued through the century the situation of Dartmoor again proved a disadvantage against the competition of other places, a decline gradually set in, and one by one the quarries closed, until today only the one at Merrivale is still in commercial production.

Probably the best known of the granite quarries, perhaps because the first railway in Devon was constructed from them, and also because they were a source of granite for London Bridge, were those at Haytor. These lie in Ilsington parish, to the north of Haytor rocks, the central one being at SX 755775. The remains of the workings, and of the rail tracks made of granite blocks, easily accessible within less than a mile of the road, are clearly visible and give an idea of the extent of activities here over a century ago.

The Haytor quarry was opened in or just before 1820, by George Templer of Stover. A necessary adjunct to the enterprise was some means of transport to take the stone away, not an easy matter in a situation such as this. Probably spurred on by the winning of a contract for supplying granite for London Bridge, special attention was paid to the problem, and a plan was devised for constructing a tramway to connect with the Stover canal at Teigngrace. The tramway was opened in September 1820 and involved a track 8½ miles in length, with a fall of around 1,300 ft. Metal rails were then unreliable and costly to transport, so the material of the quarry itself was

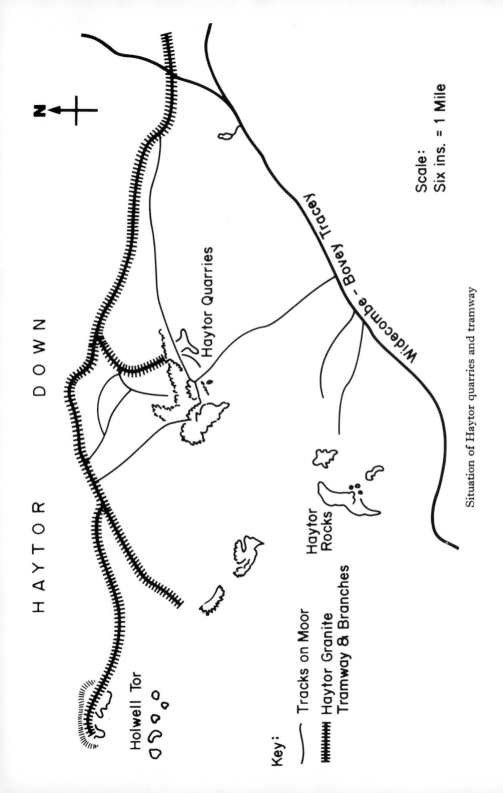

N

HAYTOR   DOWN

Holwell Tor

Haytor Quarries

Haytor Rocks

Widecombe – Bovey Tracey

Key:

——— Tracks on Moor

ㅗㅗㅗㅗ Haytor Granite
        Tramway & Branches

Scale:
Six ins. = 1 Mile

Situation of Haytor quarries and tramway

utilized and made into suitable blocks for the trackway, a most unusual idea at that time, but very suitable for the heavy loads which
were to be carried. Granite blocks roughly 1 ft square in section were
cut, with a rebate 7½ in wide and 3 in deep cut on either side. Most of
them were about 5½ ft in length, but some longer, up to about 8 ft.
Some of the joints had to be supported underneath by pieces of rock
to prevent them sinking, especially where the ground was soft. The
gauge was about 4 ft and sometimes more, there being no means of
maintaining it exactly.

The horse-drawn trucks or wagons, which could carry up to 3 tons
each, had flangeless iron wheels of 2 ft diameter, and were small and
flat, without ends or sides; the front ones usually had shafts. On one
section, that from Holwell quarry face, SX 751778, to the real beginning of the 'main' line, loaded trucks, twelve in number, had to be
drawn uphill, and for this a team of eighteen shire horses was kept.
Branches extended to the different quarry faces, with a siding at Holwell. At junctions, points were provided by the use of larger blocks
with the grooves set at an angle, and numerous short, straight blocks
were used for curves, their flanges, with wear, soon coming into
shape. The line was single all its way, except for what was probably a
spur siding near the crossing of the Manaton road, and there were no
cuttings or embankments.

The course of the railway, which started near the Holwell quarry
face, followed a general easterly direction for the first half of its
length. Traversing Haytor Down, where the branch from the main
quarry joined it, it proceeded across the Manaton road, and along
close to the one leading to Bovey Tracey. The line continued through
the Yarner estate, over Lower Down, and further on, in the vicinity
of the present pottery works, it took a south-easterly direction along
the line later followed by the Newton Abbot–Moretonhampstead
railway, to terminate at the wharf at Teigngrace.

Much of the trackway on Haytor Down, including 'points' and
branches serving the quarries, can still be traced (see plate on p. 90).
Further down the actual line can no longer be followed, though be-

low Lower Down Cross, beside Chapple Lane, a section can be seen with the setts still in place. Much of it has been removed over the years and used for other purposes; in particular a section near the Haytor–Bovey road was broken up in 1898 for use as road-making material.

The quarries were busy from their opening until the 1860s, except for a spell in the 1840s when they were leased to Johnson Bros who closed them for the advantage of their quarries on Walkhampton Common. In 1825 Haytor granite was used for the foundation stone of London Bridge, and it was employed on the bridge's west face and for blocks at each end bearing the City arms. Numerous buildings in London, including the library of the British Museum, and elsewhere in the country used granite from Haytor.

Around 1829 the railway, as well as the canal at Teyngrace, passed into the possession of the Duke of Somerset, and was worked from 1825 by the Devon Haytor Granite Company, with which was associated the building firm of Jolliffe & Banks. In 1850 the quarries were flourishing, employing about a hundred men who lived in buildings which then existed in a sheltered position flanking the tor, and in cottages by the present Rock Inn. But some time after 1865 they closed, being unable to compete with the supplies of Cornish granite which could be shipped more easily and cheaply. Some granite was used locally, but the quarries and tramline fell into disuse. Just before the turn of the century the quarries were opened again and worked for a spell by the Exeter firm of J. Easton & Son, who leased them from the Duke of Somerset. The railway, however, was no longer used, the granite being transported instead by tractor to Bovey. The last occasion on which Haytor granite, noted for its exceptional hardness, was sought was in 1919, when stone for the Exeter war memorial was cut.

In 1905 there was a plan to construct an electric tramway to take tourists up to the tor, with electricity generated by a dynamo driven by producer gas, to be obtained from burning Bovey lignite. This far-fetched attempt at commercialization of course never materialized, although the generating station had been built—it was adapted for industrial purposes.

The quarries themselves, flooded and rather smaller than one might expect, are today deserted and tranquil. With a surrounding carpet of heather and the gold of gorse, this place on many a summer's day can be a quiet retreat from the popular area of the tor rocks and car park only a short distance away. The route of the tramway has now been adapted as an amenity for walkers, and named the Templer Way.

At a number of other places on Dartmoor there are further old granite quarries. The most notable of these are on the western side, on Walkhampton Common: King Tor (SX 554739), Foggintor or Royal Oak (SX 567736) and Swell Tor (SX 560733). All are now long abandoned, but the considerable extent of the remains gives some idea of their importance during the last century. On the western side of King Tor the large holes that have been left, and some of the remains, indicate that some very large stones have been removed.

Foggintor lies about a mile along a rough track south from the Tavistock–Princetown road, which turns off almost opposite a pump-house west of Rendlestone Cross. The quarry faces here are high and cleanly cut, the area which they surround now containing a quiet pool (plate, p. 97). Beyond this are large rubble tips, including one high lengthy one striking out in the form of a headland to the north-west. There are, too, the remains of numerous buildings. Tracks from the quarry lead to the course of the old Princetown–Plymouth railway line, where there were sidings for getting the stone away. One of these tracks, continuing across the railway, leads on to the Swell Tor Quarries, little more than a ¼ mile distant, and showing some very deep workings. In making its extensive loop around King Tor during its steep ascent the railway also skirted the quarry on the south-western side, where immediate access for loading was available. Prominent still is the high embankment of the inclined plane down which the stone was conveyed from the quarry to the line.

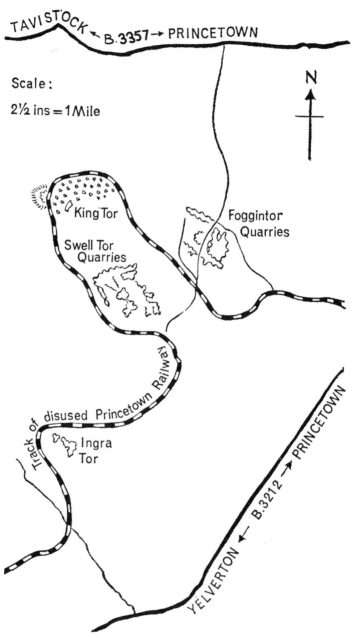

TAVISTOCK ← B.3357 → PRINCETOWN

Scale:

2½ ins = 1 Mile

N

King Tor

Foggintor
Quarries

Swell Tor
Quarries

Track of disused Princetown Railway

Ingra
Tor

YELVERTON ← B.3212 → PRINCETOWN

Disused granite quarries on Walkhampton Common

Work at these quarries was started around 1820, probably first at Foggintor, then known as Royal Oak. Even before this date a good deal of stone had been taken from this particular part of the moor for the construction of Tor Royal and some other houses in Princetown from 1785 onwards, and some years later for the building of the prison. The opening of the quarries was closely associated with the construction of the Plymouth & Dartmoor Railway, which began operating in 1823, and their working was dependent on this and the later Princetown Railway, both of which are described in Chapter Eight. The Plymouth & Dartmoor Railway Company held the lease for the granite on this part of Walkhampton Common from Sir Masseh Manasseh Lopes, but in 1823 it was assigned to the contractors for the line, Johnsons & Brice, who worked the quarries for a number of years.

Production continued at a high rate, though not continuously, through the nineteenth century, aided by the introduction of the drill. Around 1900 the quarries were in the ownership of Pethicks of Plymouth, a firm which had a contract for supplying granite for bridge work in London. At about the turn of the century work at Foggintor ceased, the company considering that the prospects at Swell Tor were better. Work continued here on a large scale and the most modern machinery of the day was used. At this time ninety men or more were employed there, living at Princetown and Rendlestone, as well as in cottages close to the quarries. Around 1920, with competition from other places and the increasing use of concrete as a building material, production declined and the workings eventually closed. Around 1937 they were reopened again for a time when waste granite was taken for use by the Devon County Council as road metal. Ingra Tor Halt on the Princetown railway was made at this stage.

A nearby competitor was the Tor Quarry, opened at Merrivale by William Duke in 1875. A great deal of high-quality granite has been taken from here over the past century. Although Mr Duke faced many difficulties in the early stages, including financial ones, the

ground work was well done and the prospects hopeful. The business
expanded, especially after 1898. After William Duke's death one of
his sons took over (his other son was the first Lord Merrivale, cabinet
minister and judge) and the firm became C. L. Duke & Co. There
was an increase in the number of men employed—in the early 1900s
about 150 and sometimes more—and the building of more houses for
the workers caused Merrivale to develop almost into a village; men
also came to work daily from Tavistock, Princetown and surrounding
villages.

The stone from Merrivale was taken by road to the railway at
Tavistock. In the earlier days the wagons were drawn by teams of
powerful horses, but in about 1901 traction engines were introduced
—to the annoyance of Tavistock District Council, who complained
bitterly of the effect the engines and their trailers had on the roads for
whose upkeep the council was responsible. In 1908 the firm applied
for permission to connect the quarry with the Princetown railway
line; in spite of some opposition this was granted, but the work was
never carried out.

In March 1903 nearly 1,600 tons of granite were blasted in one
operation, some of the rock produced being supplied to the firm of
Pethicks of the Swell Tor Quarry for part of a contract for corbels
for London Bridge[1]. At that time Merrivale was equipped with three
large steam derricks as well as a steam travelling crane. The stone
masons worked in four large sheds.

Still functioning, this quarry is now worked by a subsidiary of
Tarmac. In 1957–8 stone from it was used for the modern Merrivale
Bridge over the Walkham, and in the 1980s it was employed for the
War Memorial in the Falkland Islands.

Elsewhere on Dartmoor other nineteenth-century quarrying enterprises have left their marks. Not far from the quarries just described
was a smaller one just across the Walkham at Heckwood (SX
545738), from which stone was supplied for the Plymouth break-
water; this was transported over the canal from Tavistock to Morwellham and then shipped down the Tamar. There were small

[1]Reported in the *Western Morning News* 31 March 1903.

quarries, too, west (SX 530736) and south (SX 531732) of Pew Tor. And on the eastern side of the moor, Blackingstone Quarry was a large area of working that is no longer in commercial production.

The remains of a small quarry close to Little Trowlesworthy Tor, in Shaugh Prior parish, mark the place where a particularly fine red granite, capable of taking a high polish, was obtained during the nineteenth century, up to the 1870s or 80s. In Meavy parish, quarries near the Dewerstone were productive in the mid-nineteenth century, though closed by about 1870. A system of trackways served the workings, and remains of these can still be seen ascending the steeply rising ground, while the main track to Goodameavy is now a footpath. The tracks carried standard-gauge rails on granite sleepers and were designed to connect with the South Devon Railway, opened in 1859, by means of a high granite embankment and a bridge over the River Meavy at a point opposite Goodameavy, just north of the tunnel. This, however, was never completed, as the owner of the land refused permission to connect with the railway. Granite from the embankment was later used in the construction of the dam at Lopwell Reservoir on the River Tavy, though a quantity of it, further dissected by the tumbling of its component massive granite boulders, still remains. A. J. Allen describes in *The Western Morning News* (5 November 1962) how an inclined tramway once linked the two horizontal systems skirting the Dewerstone, controlled from a wheelhouse at the top of the incline (plate, p. 89); the rails, set in large granite sleepers, carried two parallel sets of trucks, the motive power for raising the empty trucks up the slope coming from the loaded trucks as they descended. Buildings on the lower track, which earlier served as an office and smithy, are now used as a scout adventure training centre.

At other places on the moor granite has been worked in a small way, usually for supplying local needs or for use in the construction of viaducts for the developing main railway lines. The lower slopes of Western Beacon, in the southern part of the moor, yielded granite for the viaducts at Ivybridge and Cornwood, while from a quarry near

Burrator came stone used in the dam of the reservoir there. On Brent Moor, just below the Avon dam, is the site of a quarry on the eastern side of the valley, which was also active during the nineteenth century. There are a number of others.

CHINA CLAY

An industry which has had a dramatic effect upon the scenery in the south-western part of Dartmoor, and which has been—and still is —of international economic importance, is that of china-clay extraction. Originating in the granite, of which china clay is of course a derivative, the industry has developed at places distant from the moor as well as actually on it. The ball-clay workings around Bovey Tracey, and north of the moor near Meeth, owe their occurrence to the core of Dartmoor granite, but are well outside the area, and not to be considered here. The kaolin works of Lee Moor and other places in the vicinity, however, though located largely outside the boundary of the National Park, are in typical moorland country, and cannot be separated from it.

By no stretch of imagination could the signs of clay-workings be said to enhance or blend with the moorland scene—a factor taken into consideration when the National Park boundary was being defined. The dreary white tips, more starkly prominent than any tinners' dumps, and the opaque milky whiteness of the streams and rivers flowing from them, present an eerily alien appearance. Nevertheless, few can fail to be impressed by the size of some of the tips and workings, and for the industrial archaeologist there is a certain fascination in the systems of pits, leats and tramways.

China-clay formation is due to alteration by natural forces of the structure of the granite, the felspar part having decomposed to form the fine clay or kaolin, while the other constituents, quartz and mica, have remained unchanged. On Dartmoor the industry is a comparatively recent one. The working of china clay had started in Cornwall in the eighteenth century and had expanded to meet the increasing demands of the English potteries, but not until 1830 did John Dickens and John Cawley lease some land from the Earl of Morley for the purpose of clay-working and cause the beginnings of the industry which now dominates Lee Moor. In 1833 William Phillips acquired the workings and was joined in the business two years later by his son John. Under Phillips the work went ahead at an increasing rate, and within a few years fire bricks were being made at Lee Moor, and before long also salt-glaze sanitary pipes.

By the 1870s there were nine clay works in this vicinity, which extended from Cadover Bridge south to Crownhill Down and Heddon Down, and eastwards to the source of the Tory Brook on the slopes of Penn Beacon. By this time the Lee Moor works were owned by Martin Brothers, who had taken over in 1862 and also developed pits at Wotter. Martins made considerable extensions and retained the business into the twentieth century. During these years the industrial settlement of Lee Moor grew up, and land which at the beginning of the century had been little more than bleak and barren moor, with the remains of tinners' workings, became a busy centre of habitation. Of the other firms which developed interests in this area at the end of the nineteenth century, one was Watts, Blake, Bearne & Co of Newton Abbot, who worked pits at Heddon Down, Cornwood, as well as the Wigford Down and Shaugh Lake ones further north; its activities continue today at Heddon and Shaugh Lake.

The method evolved for working the clay in the early days of the industry first necessitated the removal of the top covering of herbage or peat until the underlying decomposed rock lay exposed. This was then dug out with picks and shovels in a series of vertical steps, and a stream of water allowed to wash over the material, either actually in the pit or on its removal to some other suitable site. The water carried the solid material with it along an inclined plane and then to a series of settling pits in which the heavier sand and mica could separate out. The small clay particles continued in suspension over to the later catchment pits or ponds, where they were allowed to settle. Gradually, as the water became clearer, it was drawn off, until only the settled clay remained. This was then left to dry until sufficiently hard to be cut out, generally in 9 to 12-in cubes, after which it was taken to buildings for further drying before being sent away.

Obviously, second only to the easy availability of the actual clay-bearing material itself, the main necessity was for a ready supply of water. For the Lee Moor works water was brought from the River Plym, initially by a specially cut leat but later by adaptation of the former Bottle Hill mine leat, taken in at Ditsworthy Weir. This 4-mile leat, coming along the contours on the southern slopes of the valley and across Trowlesworthy Warren, was supplemented in the vicinity of Lee Moor by other water supplies led in from the slopes of Penn Beacon, and the Tory Brook. An adit was constructed from the clay pits to enable the water later to return to the Tory Brook and eventually the Plym.

The china-clay industry in this area, expanding and flourishing as it now is, is far from being 'archaeology'. Today's workings and modern processing plants are necessarily, to a very large extent, superimposed upon the old. However, not all the older features have been obliterated, and some are still in use.

The firm now in control of the Lee Moor workings is English China Clays International Ltd, formerly English Clays Lovering Pochin which took over from Martins in 1919. The firm's present extraction is from the three adjacent pits known as Lee Moor, Cholwich Town and Whitehill Yeo. The last two were unworked for periods earlier this century, but the working of all three is now closely integrated. With this in view, in the 1970s a new road was made from near Wotter to Tolchmoor Gate. This has had the effect of by-passing Wotter and Lee Moor villages, and has been followed by closure of a section of the old road from Cornwood.

Almost all the older structures, which comprised clay-drying buildings and chimneys, are now gone. Amongst few relics still interspersed amid modern developments is one old kiln, called the 'Klondike', used now for storing unrefined clays. The current weekly output of clay is around 8,000 tons. It is all sent in the form of a

Page 89   (above) *Parallel rectangular channels which formed part of the settling system at the clayworks near Shipley Bridge;* (below) *Cable brake drum on the incline plane at Dewerstone Quarry; photographed 1912*

Page 90　(above) *Plymouth leat, near Clearbrook;* (below) *A section of the Haytor Granite Tramway, showing 'points' leading a branch off to the right*

slurry by pipeline to the main drying works at Marsh Mills, although
some is returned in dry form to Lee Moor where it is processed in a
calciner plant for use in the rubber and plastics industries. More than
80 per cent of production is used in papermaking for filling and
coating including high gloss. Ceramics take a further 10 per cent.
Over 80 per cent of the clay is exported, some being shipped from
Cattedown Wharf, Plymouth, but most from the port of Fowey in
Cornwall. Other quantities are transported by container on cross-
channel ferries, and by train to Italy.

In former days transport of the finished product was effected by a
variety of means. A traction engine was used to transport the blocks
from Wotter to Cornwood station; clay from Heddon Down was also
carted to Cornwood, that from Crownhill Down went to Plympton.
In the case of the Shaugh Lake and Wigford Down pits, the clay in
suspension was washed down a 2-mile pipeline to a works at Shaugh
Bridge, from which the resulting clay blocks were dispatched from
the station at Bickleigh. The remains of the Shaugh Bridge drying
sheds, incompletely demolished just a few years ago, can still be seen
from the road, south of the Plym. (The route of the pipeline was a
favourite one for moorland walkers from Plymouth who used to
travel part way by train and alight at Shaugh Bridge platform.) For
the larger works at Lee Moor, a tramway was constructed to carry
clay and bricks direct to the quays at Plymouth and to bring up coal,
ironwork and general supplies.

The construction of the Lee Moor tramway was not achieved without a considerable amount of difficulty and wrangling. (A full account
of it is given by R. M. S. Hall in *The Lee Moor Tramway*.) In its
original design it was to be an extension of the Plymouth & Dartmoor
Railway (see Chapter Eight) and of Lord Morley's branch line from
this to Cann Quarry. A contract for its construction was arranged
with the South Devon & Tavistock Railway Company in 1853 as a
branch to the company's line then being built. The initial construction of the track, however, was of a very poor standard, and the
SD & T refused to take it over. Phillips tried repeatedly to get the line

into service but there were further setbacks and difficulties. However, after improvements had been made, some rebuilding done and parts of the track relaid, the tramway was at last put into operation in 1858, the SD & T company, having paid off the contractors, making a free gift of it to the Earl of Morley.

Constructed of 4 ft 6 in gauge, it is possible that some of the rails from the Plymouth & Dartmoor Railway were used. The upper sections, those serving Wotter and Cholwich Town, had track of the stone-block sleeper type. Some of the track was relaid in 1899, when locomotives were introduced over part of the way, and for this normal flat-bottomed rails were used. Over the course of its life this tramway used three different forms of motive power—horse, gravity and steam, all of them at work simultaneously on different parts of the track from 1899 until the 1940s.

The highest point on the line was at the Cholwich Town works, from where it crossed the Cornwood-Cadover Bridge road, and looped around to Lee Moor village with sidings serving the various kilns. Continuing, it was joined from the right by a tramway from the works at Wotter, and then descended the Torycombe incline, to be joined from the left by a branch from the brickworks. In its earlier days the line here crossed the Wotter Brook by means of a viaduct, but this became unsafe and was replaced in 1878 by a line around the valley to the north, along a steep, shelflike embankment. The line went into a cutting under Truelove Bridge and presently crossed the Shaugh Prior–Plympton road at Whitegates level crossing.

Through Cann Wood there was a descending incline, 1¼ mile long, with a gradient of 1 in 11, operated by cables. The system was of the counter-balanced, self-acting type; no winding engine was necessary, the descending train being the heavier and drawing up an ascending, empty train, the speed being controlled by brake-line ropes running over supports laid between the rails. The cables were fixed at the upper end to drums which revolved in drumhouses in underground chambers beneath the tracks. To overcome friction losses and to allow for the weight of the ropes it was necessary for the weight of the total load going down the incline to exceed that coming up by a minimum of 12 tons. This required careful arrangement on days when a lot of coal had to come up and the quantity of clay to go down was not large. (The Torycombe incline worked differently; water-tank wagons were used when trucks containing coal and other materials had to be hauled up.)

Below the incline the line crossed the road and a stream by a via-duct, then continued alongside the former GWR branch line. Crossing the Plym, down the Forder valley, past the entrance to the present Tecalemit factory, the line continued to Crabtree, where it crossed the road by a gateless level crossing. Further on the tramway crossed the main line on the level, went under the road, and eventually ter-minated at the Cattewater quays.

Until 1899 all traction on the line was provided by horses and the cables. But by this time the high clay output necessitated the intro-duction of two locomotives for use on the upper section, from the top of the Cann incline to the one at Torycombe, where there were sid-ings and sheds. At the same time track was laid between the two inclines, and gates were provided at the Whitegates crossing. The lower part, from the foot of the incline to the Cattewater, remained horse-drawn, the sleepers being covered with earth to give the horses easier walking. From Rising Sun to the Cattewater, the tramway in-corporated the lower section of its forerunner, the Plymouth & Dartmoor Railway. Being there before the South Devon Railway ex-tended its route from Exeter to Plymouth in 1848, the P & D had the right of way at the point where it crossed the main line, a right which the clay company's tramway continued to enjoy until 1961. No mechanical locomotion, however, was ever used on this section of the tramway, simply because horses were the only form permitted under the running powers and right of way.

When working at full capacity the tramway was capable of carrying 60,000–70,000 tons of clay annually. In 1900 the Wotter tramway was closed, when the works there changed hands, and was used as a quarry siding. 1910 saw the closure of the extension from Lee Moor village to Cholwich Town, and after 1936 traffic no longer continued on the Torycombe incline, which had served the village and quarry. After the outbreak of war, from the early 1940s transport was by motor lorries, until the laying of the Lee Moor–Marsh Mills pipeline in 1947. The railway lines have been removed, but the two locomotives (0–4–0 saddle tanks) are preserved. One, with a waggon, is at Saltram House, the other, with a signal box, is at the Wheal Martyn Museum, near St Austell, Cornwall.

As a village, the settlement of Lee Moor has remained the focal point of the clay-working area, as it was originally. It has an atmosphere of its own—one alien to the general character of Dartmoor, and more similar, in its bleakness and dustiness, to a Derbyshire limestone-quarrying village, or even, if its moon-mountainlike tips were black instead of white, to an old coal-mining area. Always dominating the scene, the white pyramids of waste on a fine day will glisten in the sun, but on a foggy November night they can look as if they themselves are fog solidified.

Not all the clayworkers reside at Lee Moor, many, as previously, come from Wotter and other localities. The nineteenth-century employers built houses for a hundred men and their families, representing a quarter of the then labour force. Many of the older dwellings have been removed to make room for extension of the main pit and modernisation, including most recently Boringdon cottages, built in 1835. A council estate, and workers' houses built by the company, and a new public hall, give an updated look to the village, which, with fewer houses, is now more compact. The Lee Moor population (largely from Cornish roots) under considerate employers had generally been regarded as close-knit and law-abiding, keen on gardening and hymn singing. Perhaps the latter is now less pronounced although the village still has its Methodist church and Anglican mission hall; there is now no school, and still, as ever, no public house. But a strong community life prevails, with numerous leisure activities—and a bar which the public hall now provides. This has never been a vicinity to which outsiders have flocked, and until the age of the motor-car Lee Moor inhabitants did not themselves travel far afield; at the turn of the century it was quite common for local families to visit Plymouth only twice a year to buy cloth and other essential goods not immediately available in the village. Isolation is far less a feature of the place now than it was formerly, the same being true of the villages of Wotter, Cornwood and Hemerdon—others which have been closely concerned, though less exclusively, in the industry of china clay.

On Brent Moor, clay was worked at Knattaburrow Pool (SX 656645) from 1836. Rosemary Robinson has described (*Plymouth Mining Club Journal* 11, 1) how the clay in suspension was conveyed in twin channels across the moor to Treeland and from there probably through pipes to a site near Glazebrook viaduct for processing. Also, from 1858 clay extracted around the source of the Bala Brook was apparently similarly conveyed to the Glazebrook site, but also from this time by the same means to refineries at Shipley Bridge, in channels cut along a route parallel to and east of the Zeal Tor tramway. The lower section of the tramway, built earlier of wooden rails bolted to granite blocks to the Redlake peatworks (see Chapter Five and p. 109) was also used for servicing the clayworks, but probably not until a later enterprise, dating from 1872 and of fairly short duration. At Shipley (SX 681629), buildings of the former naphtha works and the ground behind were adapted for treatment of the clay. On moorland above the disused buildings can still be seen rectangular and circular pits in which the mica was separated out and clay settled during the 1870s, while others to the south-west are from the 1850s workings. It has been said that the short life of clay-working on Brent Moor was due partly to the felspar being not properly decomposed, and also to mismanagement in the removal of the covering layer of peat, which dropped down and mixed with the clay.

At a later date there were also clay-works at Redlake and Leftlake, in ground around the eastern tributaries of the River Erme (Redlake at SX 646668, Leftlake at SX 647634).

The workings at Redlake were started in 1910, in spite of much local opposition during the immediately preceding years, on land leased from the Duchy of Cornwall, R. Hansford Worth being appointed engineer. In the following year the Redlake Mineral Railway was completed for carrying men, coal for the steam-pumping engines, iron and general supplies from Bittaford to the works—not for clay. Seven and a half miles long, and of 3-ft gauge, the railway terminated on the southern slopes of Western Beacon, where connection with the clay-drying plant down at Cantrell, close to the Great Western Railway, was made by cable incline (see p. 224).

The railway took a general northwards direction from Bittaford to Redlake, but wound around according to the contours of the hills. First going around the western slopes of Western Beacon and Weatherdon Hill it took a slight eastwards turn, to continue north again east of Piles Hill and between Sharp Tor and Three Barrows. Passing Leftlake, the line wound over Quickbeam Hill, across Brown Heath, and eventually reached the clay-works. Steam locomotives were used on the line, the first being a 0–4–2 side-tank type, named *C. A. Hanson* after a director of the firm. The three passenger vehicles, each capable of carrying thirty people, resembled mobile hen-houses in appearance. There were no ordinary brakes, but a centre buffer and coupling.

The clay itself was pumped from the pits by a rising main to the 'micas' at Greenhill, about a mile away. There it was allowed to settle for about a week for separation of the mica, following which the sluices were opened, and the clay suspended in water passed through a pipeline to the works at Cantrell, where the water was taken off and the resulting clay dried by baking before being dispatched on the main railway line.

About a hundred men were employed in the industry, many of whom used to stay out at the works for weeks on end during the summer, and even in winter too when the weather was not too severe. They used to supplement their food supply, and at times provide themselves with a little sport, by trapping rabbits, making warrens for them, the remains of which can still be seen at several places alongside the course of the old railway.

In 1922 an earlier china-clay works at Leftlake was reopened, necessitating a doubling of the capacity of the Cantrell works and the extension of the buildings there. Working at Leftlake suffered from the disadvantage found at Brent Moor, that of the felspar being incompletely decomposed; after a few years the clay was worked out and in 1932 the whole enterprise came to an end. By 1933 the system had been completely dismantled, the engines blown up and sold for scrap, and other equipment sold by public auction.

In the mid-nineteenth century attempts were made in various parts to develop china clay production, including the King Tor–Swell Tor area of Walkhampton Common, but without leading to commercial production.

Page 97 *The now deserted Foggintor Quarry, Walkhampton Common. Worked from around 1820–1900 the quarry supplied much granite to London, including for Nelson's column.*

CHAPTER FIVE

Peat

ANOTHER Dartmoor commodity which since ancient times has played an important part in both the domestic and industrial life of the moor is peat. It thickly blankets wide stretches of the high moor and has been valued and sought after by generations of moormen as a fuel; the scars their cutting has left behind, which it seems even time cannot always completely obliterate, are met with all over the moor.

Peat is formed by the decomposition of plant material in saturated conditions of both subsoil and atmosphere. Although the soil all over Dartmoor is of a peaty nature true peat does not occur everywhere. It is not found on the drier parts of the moor, nor even where the ground is wet if at the lower altitudes. It seems that as well as wet ground, moist air and cool temperatures are necessary for peat development, so that it is mainly found on the higher levels. The main deposits of peat accumulate where the underlying granite has decomposed, either partially to the substance known as growan, or more completely to china clay (kaolin). An instance of this can be seen at Redlake, where both peat and clay industries have existed at the same place at different times. The surroundings of the sources of the Dartmoor rivers are generally rich in peat, the elevations of over 1,200 ft above sea level assuring a high average atmospheric humidity.

There are two main areas of peat blanket bog. The larger one, to the north of the Tavistock–Moretonhampstead road, stretching away towards Okehampton, forms a watershed for a number of the principal rivers—the Taw, Tavy, Dart, Teign and many of their tributaries. In the smaller bog area to the south rise the Plym, Yealm, Erme, Avon and countless smaller streams.

A particularly good idea of the nature of the peat can be obtained in the vicinity of Cranmere Pool, around which and south as far as Fur Tor a great deal of decay of the peat bogs has occurred, reducing the once continuous layer to fragmented mounds or 'hags'. These are not due to any human activity but simply to excessive and successive weathering which has caused channels to form and the peat eventually to become drained, brittle and eroded.

The depth of the peat varies considerably; in places on Dartmoor it may be up to 20 ft, but this is exceptional. In the main the peat is much thinner, decreasing eventually to a mere peaty soil. R. Hansford Worth writes that in a survey of the Erme valley for the railway to the clayworks at Redlake no greater depth of peat than 2 ft 6 in was found until the head of the Redlake valley was reached. At this point, at an elevation of 1,400 ft, the deposits varied between 6 and 11 ft in depth.

Peat is capable of holding a very large quantity of water in proportion to the solid material of which it is formed. It also takes up moisture much more rapidly than it can lose it, so that considerable drying is necessary before it is suitable for fuel, not always easy to achieve in the moorland climate. It is in fact this difficulty which has been largely responsible for frustrating the attempts to work Dartmoor peat on an industrial scale. Nevertheless, though inferior to coal (Worth estimates 1·8–2 lb air-dried peat as equivalent to 1 lb good ordinary coal), peat was for centuries indispensable as a domestic fuel supply, and, converted to charcoal, was essential in the tin-smelting houses and for the work of the mines.

CHARCOAL FROM PEAT

The earliest industrial use of Dartmoor peat must have been by the tinners of the twelfth century as a fuel for smelting the tin ore. The taking of peat, or turbary, was one of the privileges granted the tinners by the Crown. The first charter of the stannaries, issued by King John in 1201, amongst other privileges of ancient custom, confirms 'digging tin and turves for smelting at all times'. A little later, in the reign of Henry III, a writ of 1219 commanded that men should be permitted 'to dig, burn and lead away from the Turbary of Dartmoor' peat for use in the stannaries. In 1222 the King further ordered that no one should hinder the tinners of Devon from taking fuel on the moor for their stannary, as they had been accustomed to do. Protected thus, and producing as they did such large quantities of tin, the tinners of medieval times must have been responsible for the stripping of peat from considerable areas and for some of those incursions into the surface of Dartmoor which are still visible today.

In many early records the peat is referred to as 'coal', and it seems certain that a carbonization process was devised to render the turves more suitable for smelting, capable of producing a greater heat. Considerable evidence of the burning of peat for charcoal has recently been found on the northern part of the moor and has been investigated by Mrs Diana Woolner, who has recorded her findings in *Devon & Cornwall Notes and Queries*, Vol XXX, Part IV (October 1965). Mrs Woolner estimates that activity in peat-cutting and charcoal-making for industrial purposes was spread over at least from the reign of John until the time of George IV. These operations are held responsible for the denudation of numerous large patches of the moor, in some cases the bare rock beneath having been exposed. Particular areas where this can be observed are around Kitty Tor, around and to the north-east and south-east of High Willhays, on Okement Hill and on patches further east, and along a stretch from Watern Tor south-westwards to Whitehorse Hill, with a further area to the south in the vicinity of Quintins Man. Much of the land between Wild Tor and Quintins Man has been actually lowered a number of feet.

Apart from the signs of peat cutting, evidence of the burning process has been found, in the shape of numerous mounds or 'meilers' and crude granite kilns, particularly in the proximity of Wild Tor. The humped meilers rather resemble barrows, and the kilns could be mistaken for cairns. Evidently the small blocks of peat were packed together and covered over with earth or stones, then slowly burned, under restricted and controlled air conditions, until the charcoal was formed. The resulting product was hard, rather resembling coke, and was capable of producing far greater heat than ordinary cut peat. Also, being a form of carbon free of many impurities, it was even better for smelting than was the actual coal product which eventually replaced it. Approximately 36 lb of charcoal would be produced from 100 lb of peat, so that the reduction of weight was another advantage where transport over long distances was involved. For many years men came from as far afield as Cornwall, with pack-horses, to fetch charcoal for use in the tin industry there.

In the vicinity of Whitehorse Hill and Quintins Man are the remains of some small buildings which are presumed to have been peat-cutters' shelters. One of these, called Moutes Inn, is situated 400 yd south of the summit of Whitehorse Hill, and measures approximately 12 ft × 9 ft × 5 ft 6 in. It is of dry-stone walling, now much fallen in, with a chimney, and a door facing in the direction of Varracombe. There is another hut 200 yd to the south-west, of similar dimensions but more ruinous, another larger one 400 yd south again, and a further one 200 yd north of Quintins Man of much the same size and again almost demolished.

Walking due south from Quintins Man, after crossing the North Teign, one passes a rather different sort of hut halfway up the slope, measuring about 15 ft × 6 ft × 5 ft 6 in. The chimney is at the south end and the door at the south-east corner. The exterior wall is banked and the interior filled with rushes. A little further due south again, on Marsh Hill is another, known as Stats House, which forms something of a landmark (plate, p. 108). This is very similar to the one previously described, with dimensions of 16 ft × 9 ft × 5 ft 6 in. Much of the masonry has fallen in but the chimney is clearly distinguishable.

PEAT FOR DOMESTIC USE

Except for whatever wood may have been available here and there, peat has been through the ages the moor dweller's only source of fuel. During later years, until its use ceased within living memory, the cutting and carrying of peat to the towns on the fringes of the moor was itself in the nature of a minor industry, and a source of revenue to many. In 1808 Vancouver wrote: 'Many of the minor orders of what one called farmers, derive a considerable part of their subsistence from digging and curing peat-fuel upon Dartmoor, and the commons abutting on that forest and packing it to the large towns in the South Hams.'

Turbary, or the right of forest tenants and commoners to cut and take turf from the moor for fuel, has existed from an early date. It is specifically mentioned in the Perambulation of 1240, relating to the 'turbarium de Alberysheved', a turbary situated between the South Teign and Bovey rivers. Undoubtedly the right existed even before then, and would have been fully exercised, with full advantage taken of the ample natural resources for supplying vital fuel needs in moorland dwellings. It was customary for each farm or holding to have its own turf-tie or place on the moor where the occupier had his established appropriation of the peat-cutting; the rule was that each moorman kept to his own tie and did not interfere with those of anyone else.

Peat-cutting was summer work done at any time between the end of April and early September. The practice was to work in long strips or 'journeys' which were commonly 40 yd in length, two turves wide and 18 or 20 in deep. As successive journeys were worked, parallel with each other, the turf-tie took on the appearance of a large rectangular pit. Sometimes the depth would increase to several feet, and generally the deeper the cutting the better fuel the peat would make. Usually a peat-tie would continue to be worked for a considerable number of years, the excavated area extending all the while, until either the supply became exhausted or the limit of the individual's area was reached. On the moor today the sites of old peat-ties of this sort can frequently be seen. Usually they are grown over and almost indiscernible from the surrounding moor, the only clues to their existence being the alterations of level and the fairly regular lines. After the peat had been removed, care was in fact taken to replace the top turve, in order to preserve the herbage.

Special tools were used, consisting of a long slitting-knife or slicer and a budding-iron, which prepared the ground, and a turf-iron with which the actual peat removal was performed. The long knife, 2½–3 ft in length, 3–4 in wide and fitted to a wooden handle, was used firstly for trimming off the edge of the previous year's cut before the new season's work commenced, and then for making the initial cut

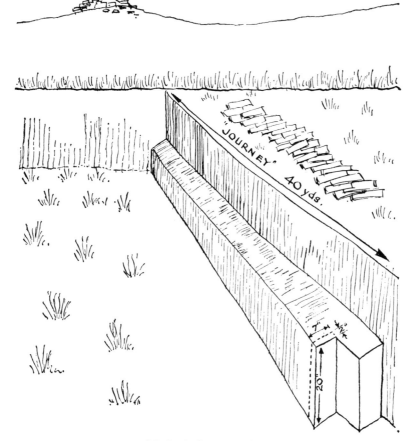

Method of peat-cutting

deep into the peat, at a distance of 14 in from the edge, along the
length of the next journey. Next came the removal of the covering
layer of soil and vegetation; if shallow this was done with a shovel, but
if deep (and sometimes there could be as much as 2 ft of soil) resort
was made to the budding-iron, a tool resembling a shovel, but triangular in shape and flatter, with a straight handle. The worker would
stand down in the turf-tie, pushing the budding-iron horizontally
into the side of the trimmed face at the upper level of the new peat,
taking off the layer of soil and throwing it back behind him into the
tie, the growing herbage being preserved to place on top. When this
was completed all the way along the peat lay denuded and the actual
cutting could commence.

The cutting was done with the turf-iron, a piece of flattened iron
7 in wide with a slightly sharp-edged rounded end. Along one side a
pointed triangular extension was bent upwards at right angles. The
top end of the iron was formed into a rounded socket to take the
wooden handle, with a 'shoulder' at right angles to enable foot pressure to be applied when cutting down into the peat. Walking back-
wards along the new journey, the operator would introduce the turf-
iron into the peat 2 in from the end, and make a series of short vertical downward cuts, keeping the cut material in one piece, until a
depth of 20 in was reached. The upright 'horn' at the side of the turf-
iron assisted in cutting out the square-edged section. Finally, when
at the required depth, a slight horizontal nick was made, when the
whole slab, 20 in × 7 in × 2 in, would come away.

A double row would be cut in this way along the 14-in width for
the length of the journey, the pieces from one side being placed in the
tie, those from the other side being put up on the uncut ground. An
industrious man would cut two such journeys a day.

The resulting pieces of peat would then be stood up against each
other in pairs for drying to commence, after two or three weeks being
stooked several to a group, or were laid out beside the journey. When
weather conditions had allowed sufficient drying, the peat was collected and taken to the vicinity of the farmhouse, where it was

stacked in a rick and later thatched. In the earlier days it was carried on the backs of ponies aided by a wooden appliance known as a crook. Later, horse-drawn carts were used, and a line of these, winding their way along an ancient track from the turf-ties, was a frequent sight on an autumn day, and no doubt a welcome one with the thought of the approach of the Dartmoor winter. Up to forty cartloads would be required to supply the year's needs of the farmhouse.

The peat taken to the towns and villages around the moor for sale was usually carried in heavily loaded panniers on horses or often donkeys. With the advance of the railways coal became easily available to the former customers, and by about 1900 the trade had almost disappeared, though peat was still being used in considerable quantities by the moor dwellers themselves. Well-dried peat gave a good, steady, even heat and by putting the ashes back on top of the fire at night it could be kept alight until morning. The atmosphere of the moor in those days was constantly charged with the pleasant aroma of peat fumes from the dwellings.

On the borders of the moor, beyond the extent of the actual peat deposits, slabs of ordinary turf were cut for fuel and treated in the same way as the peat. These were known as 'vags'.

COMMERCIAL PEAT WORKING

During the nineteenth century the peat in certain areas of Dartmoor was also worked on a more commercial basis. Generally these enterprises were started optimistically, with high hopes for a lucrative future, but they were mostly short-lived, the rigorous conditions proving again and again that no easy profit could be grasped by scratching the back of the moor.

It was, however, not with illusions of a quick direct profit, but more from necessity, that the Walkham Head peatworks (SX 575807 etc) was developed. From these workings, around the sources of the River Walkham and the Eastern Red Lake (a tributary of the Tavy) in a remote part of the north-western sector of the moor, were supplied large quantities of peat for use in the mines at Mary Tavy, about 5 miles to the west—in particular Wheal Betsy, on Black Down, where lead was mined and smelted, and Wheal Friendship nearby. The peat was carried by pack-horses along a track known as Black Lane (the adjective 'black' on the moor often refers to an association with peat) which led from the cutting areas along the slopes of Lynch Tor, south of Standon Hill, and, by way of Bagga Tor Gate, off the moor and to the vicinity of the mines. Peat from this source was still being used in large quantities at the mines in the 1840s, but in later years was replaced with coal. The turf-ties around Walkham Head were occasionally later reworked—at one stage around 1880—but on a much smaller scale.

Other areas to the north of the Tavistock–Two Bridges road were, in the nineteenth century, worked for the peat used for the making of naphtha at Princetown. There is an average of about 65 per cent of volatile matter in peat, and by a process of distillation it is possible to extract the inflammable material known as naphtha. In 1844 Peter Adams and Jacob Hall Drew started a naphtha works at Bachelor's Hall, removing two years later to the vacant war prison. The supplies of peat were brought from the northerly setts at Greena Ball, Holming Beam and Fice's Well on a tramway, in trucks 10 ft square at the top, made of steel and iron, drawn by horses. The firm, known as the British Patent Naphtha Company, extracted the oils from the peat, and produced candles and mothballs as well as gas for lighting purposes. Paper was also manufactured as a sideline from the fibrous upper layers of peat, over 30 tons of peat being used per day. The Prince Consort paid a visit to the works when at Princetown in 1846.

During its short life the industry provided work for a number of local people out at the ties during the summer. Cutting started at the end of April and continued until the first Wednesday in September, which was Princetown Fair day. The turves were dug to a depth of 5 to 7 ft, women and children helping to carry them out to be at intervals turned, stooked and stacked, and eventually put on the tramway for Princetown. In spite of all efforts, however, the venture—which

Page 107 (above) *One of the numerous large rocks on the slopes of Staple Tor which bear marks of having been split—in this case the attempt was apparently not completely successful;* (below) *'Bankers' used by nineteenth-century granite sett makers here*

Page 108   (above) *The remains of Stats House, a peat-cutters' shelter, on Marsh Hill, south of Quintins Man;* (below) *Peat cut and laid to dry near Beardown Tor in the early years of the present century*

including the tramway had cost £19,000—proved uneconomic and ceased after but a few years.

Later, in the 1870s, peat cut by convicts was used, after drying and storing, in the making of gas by which, for a number of years, the prison was lit.

Another naphtha works was in operation at about the same time as the Princetown one, situated by the River Avon at Shipley Bridge, on the southern edge of the moor. The pioneers of this project were Messrs Davy & Wilkin, of Totnes. In 1846 they leased land near Redlake Mire from the Duke of Cornwall, with the right of 'cutting, manufacturing and vending peat and peat charcoal'. They constructed the Zeal Tor tramway, of wooden rails bolted to granite blocks, which ran in a south-easterly direction from Redlake across Brent Moor to Shipley Bridge. Along this the peat was transported in horse-drawn trucks. The whole system started to operate in 1847, but only survived a few years. The two partners were also concerned at the time with the Ashburton Gas Works, so the two businesses may have been connected in some way. In 1850 the partnership was dissolved, Davy paying Wilkins £4,000, and so ended another fruitless attempt at industrializing the moor.

The men who worked in the peat-cutting at Redlake used to stay out there the full week, returning to their homes, most of which were at South Brent, only at weekends. They built themselves a house of sorts on Western White Barrow, and lived largely on rabbits poached from nearby Huntingdon Warren.

Much of the route of the old tramway can still be seen (see p. 221); the lower part of it was later, in 1872, used by the Brent Moor Clay Company (see Chapter Four), as also was the building at Shipley, now demolished.

At Rattlebrook Head, in the north-western part of Dartmoor, was another peatworks. This one, started probably around the 1850s, was sustained intermittently over almost a century, up to quite recent times. The interesting, and at times almost fantastic history of the Rattlebrook peatworks seems to be a record of alternating enthusiasms and frustrations. Situated about 4 miles, as the crow flies, north-east of Lydford village, the remains of the peatworks lie in a boggy area, the source of the Rattlebrook, a tributary of the Tavy, between Great Links Tor and Amicombe Hill (SX 559872). As with so many of Dartmoor's abandoned industrial sites, it is hard to believe that this remote place, where today the whistle of the wind, the singing of the larks overhead and the gurgle of the stream are the only sounds, and sheep farmers and moor-walkers, foxes and rabbits the only visitors, was once a busy scene involving trucks on rails, ovens and chemical processes.

Though there was undoubtedly activity here earlier, first Duchy of Cornwall records of peat operations at Rattlebrook Head date from 1868. Ten years later, in 1878, the Duchy granted a licence to the West of England Compressed Peat Company Ltd to work 1 square mile of the area for £100 per annum, merging into one-twentieth dues, with the right to construct a tramway. The company, the directors of which were mainly Exeter business men, had been incorporated in the previous year, with £50,000 capital in £5 shares. Its aim was to convert the 'vast' peat beds of Dartmoor into fuel by a process of hydraulic compression invented by Mr John Howard, FRGS, of Topsham. It was said that the fuel could be supplied at half the cost of coal, and would also be suitable for producing gas and for smelting and fertilizing. In the September of 1878 the first sod of the railway was cut by the High Sheriff of Devon, Mr Hamlyn, with a silver spade. The august assembly on that occasion, which included mayors, aldermen, magistrates and a representative of the Duchy, contributed a number of flowery and optimistic speeches. An officer of the Royal Navy, Captain Peacock, belying the senior service's reputation for extreme caution in the face of innovation, said that if the navy's steam vessels burnt peat instead of coal it might be a way of reducing the Navy Estimates.

In 1879 the railway, of standard 4 ft 8½ in gauge, was completed to connect with the London & South Western Railway, at a cost of £6,000. The 5-mile line followed a steep and tortuous route from

Bridestowe station to the peatworks, for in that distance it had to ascend nearly 1,000 ft, from 800 to 1,750 ft above sea level. After leaving the station the railway crossed the Tavistock–Okehampton road (A386) close to the point where the road bridge crosses the main railway line. It then swept due southwards over Southerly Down, presently to turn northwards again above the valley of the Lyd, skirting the western slopes of Great Nodden, and on to its most northerly point, on the slopes of Corn Ridge (plate, p. 115). Here there was a reversing point and a short level; the wagons were run in and stopped for the points to be changed, and the horses moved to what had been the rear end of the train, before the ascent was continued. The track then followed a south-easterly direction, beneath Gren Tor and Hunt Tor, before a final run-in eastwards (plate, p. 125). In the earliest days the trucks on this railway were drawn by horses, but in its later years it was mechanized. From its terminus at the peatworks short lengths of narrow-gauge track extended to the workings, and the trams on these were either drawn by horses or pushed by the men themselves.

In spite of its enthusiastic beginning, in 1880 or soon after the venture failed, after a large quantity of peat had been removed, and work stopped. The failure was partly due to the high cost of the railway, which it had been thought was going to ensure success. During the next twenty years a number of mainly unsuccessful efforts were made to resume operations. Around 1884 a spectacular enterprise was started, extracting the moisture from the peat by a process of evaporation. The peat was cut into small blocks which were fed into a machine which periodically turned them over while hot air was being blown through. Entering the machine as large as bricks and as soft as putty the pieces came out dry and the size of a man's finger. Again the project was short-lived, and failed in about 1887. It is reputed that in another attempt in the 1890s by a German scientist some success was achieved for a time, but that the secret died with the scientist.

At about the turn of the century, however, the outlook appeared rather brighter, and there were high hopes that the industry would really flourish. In about 1901 work restarted, progressing fairly

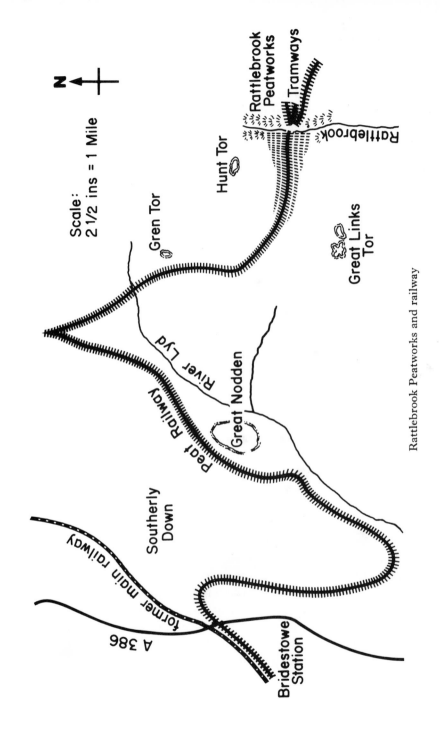

Rattlebrook Peatworks and railway

Scale:
2 1/2 ins = 1 Mile

N

Gren Tor

Hunt Tor

Rattlebrook
Peatworks

Tramways

Rattlebrook

Great Links
Tor

River Lyd

Peat Railway

Great Nodden

Southerly
Down

former main railway

A 386

Bridestowe
Station

steadily until the Great War, eight or nine men being employed at a time on cutting the peat. The work was not continuous, but would be done in spells of several weeks at a time winter or summer; local people were glad of the employment, as it was the only industry for miles around, apart from farm work. The men would make the daily climb to Rattlebrook Head from Sourton and other points in all weathers; conditions of work were tough, and sometimes, when the weather deteriorated during the day, the men's return journey would be a battle against freezing rain, fog or snow.

The tools used at Rattlebrook Head, and the size of the resulting block of peat, varied slightly from those more generally standard on other parts of the moor, as did the length of the 'journey'. Slabs were cut of 18 in downward length, but instead of being 7 in wide by 2 in thick, they were 4 in in both breadth and depth; the turf-iron was correspondingly smaller (plate, p. 125). The length of a journey at Rattlebrook was twenty paces, three turves wide, the equivalent of 60 yd of turves in all. The men were paid 2s a journey when on piece-work, and at other times 17s a week.

Drying was as ever the great problem and various methods were tried. Exposure to the moorland air, moisture-laden as it so frequently is, was realized to be insufficient, and at one stage a pressing process was attempted; this was abandoned because it was found that not only the water, but much of the peat itself, was squeezed out. Large ovens, using charcoal, were constructed, but even these were not fully effective.

Besides the use of the black peat as fuel, the grey peat was also used as a bedding for horses, and several attempts were made to use peat for various other purposes. From 1917 to 1919 further efforts were made to work the deposits, a German scientist by the name of Muller being employed, and investigations were made in the hope of extracting all kinds of useful chemical substances. Some experiments involving the use of great heat were tried, but apparently without much success; always the difficulties were the high water content and the process of drying. In 1921 a visit was paid to the Rattlebrook works by the then Prince of Wales, following which he descended to Bridestowe on the railway which now had light petrol-driven locomotives. The rails were not to survive much longer; with almost complete cessation of work, they were removed in the 1930s.

This, however, was still not the end of the story. In 1936 a licence was granted by the Duchy to Holford Processes Ltd of London to work 360 acres of peat at Rattlebrook for the production of oil, charcoal and chemical by-products, together with 6 miles of the rail-less railway track leased partly from the Duchy and partly from Major Calmady-Hamlyn. It was estimated that each ton of peat would yield at least 50 gallons of crude oil and it was aimed to produce 35,000 gallons a week, eventually rising to 100,000 gallons. Work was done on repairing the old buildings, rebuilding the route of the old railway as a vehicle track and installing plant. The works and plant, including a retort to deal with 50 tons of peat a day, were to cover an acre of ground and in 1937 the firm planned to pipe oil direct to Devonport. In spite of a number of difficulties, which included considerable opposition on amenity and water-supply grounds, and lack of financial support, Holford Processes started work in 1943. But it soon stopped: the country was then in the middle of the second world war, and this part of the moor was inaccessible due to military activities. In 1946 further experiments were carried out, and during ten months of that year 8,500 cu yd of peat were cut. A very wet summer produced an exceptionally heavy water content in the peat, however, and with the high cost of haulage the result was a financial disaster.

During the national fuel crisis of March 1947 the Ministry of Fuel & Power reviewed the possibility of peat being used in homes and industry. Dartmoor was especially considered, but it was decided that the scheme would be uneconomic and impossible. In 1951 permission was given to the Christow Manufacturing Company to take up to 2,500 tons of peat a year, and in 1952 there were plans for introducing a baking plant, the peat to be used for agricultural purposes. Again the result was failure.

From 1955 the peatworks were let for a time to Messrs Renwick,

Wilton & Dobson. For a while this firm extracted the peat and sold it, granulated, solely for horticultural purposes. But this came to an end as the business proved to be uneconomic, and the Duchy has not issued a further lease.

As a final indignity, when in recent years local farmers whose stock graze this part of the moor feared that the buildings were becoming a possible danger to animals sheltering from the weather, the Commoners asked the Duchy to demolish them. Even this presented something of a problem, due to the remoteness and the great thickness of the stone walls. The Duchy requested the army's assistance, and they were blown up in 1961.

Apart from the long line of scars over the area where the peat was cut, only heaps of rubble, rusted metal and portions of incompletely demolished walls now remain at Rattlebrook Head. The walls were about 4 ft thick and dated probably from the earliest days of working. White bricks were also used in construction and a number of these marked 'Martin Leemoor' still lie around. The track of the railway can be easily traced.

Page 115 *Embankment of the former Rattlebrook peat railway. The route ascended nearly 1,000 ft over a winding 5 miles to the peatworks, which lay in the dip beyond Great Links Tor.*

CHAPTER SIX

Mills and Miscellaneous

THROUGH the ages other forms of industry have been represented over Dartmoor and its immediately surrounding region. Water being until modern times a most important source of power, it is only to be expected that, in an area so well blessed with tumbling streams, mills should have been set up not only to supply the basic necessities of life but also to serve the purposes of thriving trades. It is often hard to realize, in the highly powered mechanical world of today, what a very real asset the abundant water of Dartmoor was as a source of energy. This abundance, coupled with the velocity it gathered in its fall from the moorland heights, once harnessed by man's ingenuity to turn one or a succession of wheels, provided power that was both cheap and reliable.

From ancient times there were, of course, the corn mills. Also originating from an early date were the woollen industries once centred in a number of the border towns and villages. Then, in more recent times, there existed small edge-tool factories on the eastern fringes, and even some of Devon's paper-making trade verges on the Dartmoor areas. Almost in the middle of the moor are the considerable remains of a gunpowder factory; and various other small productive industries grew up at different points on the borders.

Besides its use for direct power, water has been extracted from the moor for the supplying of human needs, and ancient leats constructed for this purpose can still be seen. Hydro-electric schemes of more modern times also have aspects of industrial archaeological interest where they have used mill or mine leats of earlier days. The leats, indeed, were of no less importance than the mill buildings or mines which drew power from them. It is almost impossible to walk very far on Dartmoor without coming across one of the numerous leats which cut across its surface, rounding a hillside like a tangible contour line. Some of these are barely discernible, devoid now of water, their sides broken in and beds overgrown. A few still show signs of constant attention, full of water still flowing quietly, mysteriously and purposefully, either to fulfill its original function or to perform some newer task.

Reliable water supplies were jealously guarded by parishes having rights to them. South Tawton has a leat thought to have been made in the thirteenth century; water from it was extracted from the Blackaton Brook on the border of Throwleigh parish, and by arrangement with the owner of Frog Mill the parish of South Tawton was allowed the stipulated volume of an 'ox-bow' of water, though the exact meaning of the term in this connection is somewhat obscure. The leat ran north through the parish of North Tawton and South Zeal village to join the River Taw at Taw Green, having on its way served the local mills, as well as providing power for the limestone quarries. (This leat has the interesting incidental effect of diverting northwards to the Bristol Channel waters in Barnstaple Bay, a flow which by nature would have gone to the English Channel.)

This sort of system also existed at other places around the moor; Sticklepath had in the eighteenth century at least seven mills worked by water from the River Taw, all in close proximity to the village street, and some of these were in operation until recent times. Chagford mills were dependent on water from the River Teign, while in the south the little River Ashburn, which gave its name to Ashburton, became known alternatively as the Yeo, a term used in this region to describe a river or stream from which a leat is taken. The Ashburn— or Yeo—was certainly of prime importance to the town of Ashburton; in 1605 seven mills there were powered by its water.

CORN MILLS

Mills for grinding corn, for flour or grist (stock feed), were exceedingly numerous, some of them existing from medieval times when they superseded the use of hand querns. It was usual for each manor to have its own grinding mill, to which all the people who worked on the manor would be required to bring their corn. The main mill on the moor itself was at Babeny (SX 673752), beside the Walla Brook, though now no longer standing. It was said to have been newly built in 1302 and the dwellers on the Forest of Dartmoor were obliged to grind their corn there.

As in other parts of the country the mill was an essential part of local life and some Dartmoor parishes could boast more than one. Many of the old mills have in recent times fallen into disrepair, though some of the buildings are maintained and put to other uses—some have been converted to attractive dwelling houses, like those at Jordan (Widecombe), Furlong (Drewsteignton) and Meavy. At least one, Sandypark (Chagford), is now a hotel, and others, like those at Rushford (Chagford), Gidleigh, and Lurgecombe (Ashburton) are now used for agricultural purposes. In some, including Peter Tavy Higher Mill and Batworthy (Chagford), parts of the machinery are still preserved in original buildings.

In a few instances a wheel is still *in situ*, in some cases having been rebuilt for use in generating electricity, as at Holy Street and Yeo Mills (Chagford) (see p. 192) and Bagtor (Ilsington). Often the leat is still capable of carrying water.

Most of the mills were in use for grinding corn until earlier years of the present century. Some survived until just before or shortly after the second world war, since when their work has been taken over by the large commercial firms.

WOOLLEN MILLS

Down through the ages the woollen industry has featured in the history of Dartmoor, but far more prominently in that of Devon as a whole. The significance of Dartmoor has been as an area on and around which sheep have abounded for centuries, and also as a source of water, necessary both to provide power and for the washing of the wool. Possessing these two essentials the Dartmoor border area, not surprisingly, has played its full part in the wool trade of Devon.

The early moor dwellers certainly kept sheep and there is evidence that they knew how to spin. For centuries the industry was a domestic one, all the operations of combing, spinning and weaving being carried out in or near the people's houses. The women and the children as well would work at the trade and through Elizabethan times and up to a century ago almost every cottage in the neighbourhood had its spinning wheel or loom. Raw wool was received in the cottages either direct from the farmer, or else through a master comber or spinner who bought in the market and distributed to those who worked for him. The spun wool would later be bought by a master weaver—or webber—who again distributed to the operators of looms, or in some cases, particularly in later times, had his own team of apprentices working directly under him on his own premises. Individual weavers would sell the roughly woven cloth to the master of the fulling or tucking mill in which the cloth was further treated by washing, dyeing and finishing. Tucking mills were situated in nearly all the towns and large villages around the moor.

During the eighteenth century the woollen industry in Devon showed a general decline, caused partly by the wars of that time and also by the rise, in the latter half of the century, of a better organized industry elsewhere, notably in Yorkshire, which had the advantages of coal, mechanization and a developing factory system. Many towns in Devon withdrew from the woollen industry at this stage, though some of those around the moor managed to keep it going, by taking advantage of the newer methods, if only for a time. Most of the old woollen mills have been either demolished or converted for some other use.

Of the places which survived until the later days, Chagford was one. Large woollen mills had been established here by Mr Berry of Ashburton in 1800, worked by water power supplied by a leat taken off the River Teign just below Holy Street. The main portion was contained in two large buildings at Factory Cross (SX 694878), with a tucking mill at the Lower Factory (SX 697879), and a drying store on the site of the Moorlands Hotel. In Rack Field, near Factory Cross (SX 695877), there used to be a 300 ft long drying shed which blew down in a gale on 20 February 1861. Blankets and serge were made and waggoners used to take the coarse woollen serges across the moor to Ashburton and Buckfastleigh, returning with loads of lime. One hundred and twenty men worked at the Chagford mills in those days, summoned to work by a bell which was later removed to the chapel at Postbridge.

The business declined during the middle years of the century and closed in 1848, but became active again when taken over by a Mr Vicary from North Tawton, who was also instrumental in building a gasworks nearby for providing light. Around 1880 work again closed down and the buildings lay disused. In 1890 the Higher Factory was taken over by Mr G. H. Reed, who used it for saw-milling and crushing oats. Reed floated a company and converted the mill to generate hydro-electricity using the factory's old wheel (see p. 139). The original building has since been demolished, its site occupied now by the premises of the Central Electricity Generating Board. The former Lower Factory is now converted into flats.

At only one place does wool processing survive, at Buckfast, near Buckfastleigh. Buckfastleigh retained its own mill until recently and its situation where Dartmoor's southern slopes give way to sheltered combes and rich farm land, undoubtedly played a part in the establishment of its woollen industry, and the geographical advantages must also have some bearing on its continued representation. Besides lying in traditional sheep country, carrying hill types on the moor and long-woolled breeds in the valleys, the parish has the waters of both the Dart and one of its tributaries, the Mardle, flowing through it. To these long, winding rivers, with their soft peaty waters so suitable for washing the wool, and as sources of power, the town must owe almost as much as to the proximity of the sheep.

In the middle of the twelfth century the Cistercian monks came to

Buckfast Abbey; they encouraged the industry there and also built up an export trade. The so-called 'Abbot's Way' across Dartmoor, from Buckfast to the abbeys at Buckland Monachorum and Tavistock, was in days gone by known by the moormen as the 'Jobber's Way' or 'Jobber's Path', because of the yarn jobbers who used it, their pack-horses loaded with wool yarn.

Little is recorded about the industry's history at Buckfastleigh during the next few hundred years, but it must have continued, as it did in other places all over the county. Possibly it was overshadowed by the woollen centres at Ashburton and Totnes, each just a few miles away and thriving. Somehow Buckfastleigh managed to survive the decline of the wool trade which overtook most of Devon in the eighteenth century, the selling of serge to the East India Company for the Chinese market until 1833 no doubt helping to keep the in-dustry alive through the difficult years. But even after this date it was, in fact, rising in importance compared with other places. In 1838 there were 700 looms at Buckfastleigh, more than in any other town in the county, and almost a quarter of all the remaining ones in Devon.

In 1817 a worsted spinning frame had been set up at Buckfast and the introduction of other mechanical devices was soon to change the character of the trade in the vicinity. Up to the middle of the nine-teenth century wool-combing was the occupation of many of the people of Buckfastleigh; there were eighteen master-combers em-ploying 300 people in 1850, but the development of machinery was to put these individual employers gradually out of business.

In 1806 Joseph Hamlyn had bought a tannery at Buckfastleigh, and with his three sons had engaged in fellmongering there—buying sheepskins and selling the wool and pelts separately. Later they began hand-combing at the tannery, but in 1842 they rented premises at West Mill for this branch of their work, until in 1846 they bought the Town Mill beside the River Mardle, where the present woollen mill now stands (SX 737662). The Town Mill had previously been called 'Sage's' and was believed to have been in earlier days a stamping-mill for ores from nearby mines. Here the Hamlyns installed their first combing machine. Also at this stage they bought and used Higher Buckfast Mill, said to have been on the site of the ancient one of the Cistercian monks, latterly a plating works (see p. 190 and plate on p. 126).

At the Buckfastleigh Town Mills cloth manufacturing was developing, using locally grown wool as the raw material, and in 1896 a limited company was formed, with a capital of £200,000. The wool was collected from a wide area around, and every day men would go out with pony-traps and horse-drawn wagons to the various farms, many of them situated in the wildest parts of the moor.

White's directory of 1878 records five blanket, serge and combing mills in the parish, giving employment to 100 people. The largest of these was that of Messrs Berry, started at Buckfast in about 1850 after removal from Ashburton. Though burnt down in 1877, causing a loss of £40,000 and throwing 450 people out of work, rapid rebuilding was soon in progress.

At the turn of the century the population of Buckfastleigh was around 4,000—50 per cent more than today. The great source of employment was the wool trade, Hamlyns being the largest of the four mills. In 1920 the business was bought by the Co-operative Wholesale Society, which continued wool manufacture here until 1974. Soon afterwards several of the old buildings beside the Mardle to the north of Chapel Street were demolished, together with the familiar tall chimney. Just two of the former (1800s) main blocks survive. Premises sold by the CWS to Teignbridge District Council are now let to various individuals who have small enterprises, including pastry cooking, and light engineering. The fellmongery and tanning industries continue, with sheepskins now being brought from many parts of the country.

At Buckfast, the business formerly that of John Berry & Co still continues. Here for many years were made blankets and serge. The blankets were of fine quality and rows of these, hung up in a field beside the Dart to dry in the sun after making and treatment, were at one time a familiar local sight. Until recently, blankets, cloth and travelling rugs were still being made, but the Buckfast Spinning Company, which acquired the business from Berrys in 1950, is now solely concerned with spinning yarn for carpet manufacture. (See p. 190).

EDGE-TOOL MILLS

There have also been on the Dartmoor borders edge-tool mills, making different kinds of metal tools for agricultural purposes.

One of these was the Finch Foundry situated at Sticklepath, close beside and to the south of the old Okehampton–Exeter road as it passes through the village. The original building on this site was known as Manor Mills and was already well established by the eighteenth century; at that time it was apparently used in two sections, one being a corn mill and the other a mill for woollen cloth. In 1814 Mr Finch occupied the cloth mill and converted it for the production of agricultural tools, and scoops for the china-clay industry. Eventually, as trade increased, the corn mill was also incorporated, and the business continued in the ownership of successive generations of the Finch family, of whom at one time nine members were working at the foundry together, until production ceased in 1960. The business was an important feature of life in Sticklepath, providing employment for up to twenty men until the second world war. The articles made included paring-hooks of numerous sizes and shapes, hammers, picks, choppers, hay-knives, axes and hoes; all were of fine quality and had a high reputation throughout the south-western counties. During the 1950s the business declined, partly due to competition from mass-produced products and also because of a diminished demand for hand-tools on farms, as machinery took over.

For some years the buildings sank into dereliction, the interior a confusion of fallen masonry, timbers and belting. Then, in the 1960s, due to the interest and initiative of succeeding family members, restoration of the foundry was begun. A charitable trust was set up for the preservation of the buildings and machinery, which were regarded as being of considerable historic and educational value. Following a full survey, and the receipt of donations from private and public bodies, including the Pilgrim Trust, the work went ahead. Voluntary labour, including that of students, played a large part in the restoration, which initially involved repair of the leat from the River Taw to the waterwheels.

On completion of the restoration the Finch Foundry was opened to the public, and it is now recognised as a notable museum of industrial history. The three waterwheels have been restored to working order and can be seen in operation. One drives a fan providing the air blast to the various furnaces and forges. The second gives power to a pair of heavy tilt hammers. The third waterwheel drives a large grind-stone for sharpening the tools produced (at which the men worked lying face down on a bench), a polisher wheel and a wood-cutting band-saw. In two galleries are displayed a depiction of the use of water for power, and a collection of the hand tools made at the premises, and other associated artefacts.

Another edge-tool mill, at Steps Bridge, on the River Teign near Dunsford, was probably founded about 200 years ago, though its origins may have been even earlier. The place was formerly known as Iron Mills, and some halberds dug up on the site may indicate that these were originally made here. Active business in the manufactur-ing of a wide range of horticultural and agricultural hand-tools still continues under Messrs A. Morris & Sons Ltd, in the modernised premises on the south side of the Exeter–Moretonhampstead road (B3212), east of the river. The waterwheel which formerly operated two tilt hammers is still in position and can be seen from the road (plate, p. 126). It was installed in 1821 and, although it fell into disrepair in 1937, it has now been restored to working order.

PAPER MILLS

The southern and eastern border areas of Dartmoor have carried a representative share of Devon's paper mills since the industry be-

Page 125 (above) *Looking down the last few yards of the disused railway track to the abandoned Rattlebrook Peatworks;* (below) *A turf-iron (for a left-handed worker) of the type and size used specifically at Rattlebrook; held by the late Mr Walter Alford, who himself cut peat at Rattlebrook*

Page 126   (above) *Higher Buckfast Mill, latterly a plating works and formerly a woollen mill. A large wooden launder still carries water along the rear of the building; formerly this turned the waterwheel, later was used for generating electricity; (below) The original waterwheel at the edge-tool mill at Steps Bridge. Installed in 1821, it fell into disrepair in 1937 but has now been restored to working order.*

came established in the county in the middle of the eighteenth century. The conditions which the paper industry demanded—clear water for the manufacturing process and for power, and an easy supply of raw materials—were readily met from the moorland rivers and streams and from the proximity of the port of Plymouth; the latter, besides giving access to the necessary supplies of rags and hemp, also provided a market for the product and the facilities for export.

There were half a dozen or so paper mills in this part of Devon, of which only one, that at Stowford, beside the River Erme at Ivybridge, still operates today. Probably the earliest was one near Shaugh Prior which is believed to have existed from 1756 to 1832, and to have contained two vats in 1783. Others being worked around this time were at South Brent, from 1766 to 1832, and at Town Mills, Moreton-hampstead, from 1766 to 1826; here, in 1776 there were ten hammers in use for making pasteboard, used for the packing of the bales of serge. Another paper works operating in the 1790s was at Phoenix Mill, near Horrabridge (see p. 199). Others, which grew up at the end of the eighteenth or early in the nineteenth centuries, installed machines and survived into the present century. There were two at Ivybridge, another at Lee Mill Bridge, and one at Buckfastleigh. Of these, the small one at Lee Mill which had started in 1833 was burnt down in 1908, Buckfastleigh ceased paper production in 1942 and the lower Ivybridge Mill closed in 1906. The premises of both (outside this area of study) are now used for other trades.

Various factors brought about the decline of the industry in these parts—the use of alternative materials in the form of esparto grass and wood pulp which the south-west was not so well placed for importing, the concentration of industry in other parts of the country nearer the coalfields, and foreign as well as home competition. The spread of the railways, which favoured some mills to the detriment of others, was another important influence and one which played a considerable part in the retention of the industry at Ivybridge, through which, in 1848, came the line of the South Devon Railway linking Plymouth with London.

The original mill at Stowford, Ivybridge, was built in 1787 by William Dunsterville of Plymouth and in its early days was known as 'Stowford Lodge Paper Mills'. Little is known of its early history though it is certain that hand-made white paper was produced there until the installation of a 40-in Fourdrinier machine in 1837. This advance to machinery was another reason for the survival of the industry at Ivybridge at a time when many Devon paper mills were going out of business. In 1849 John Allen bought the mill as a speculation and under him the business grew considerably. In the 1860s two 72-in Fourdrinier machines were installed and a large building programme undertaken. Allen died in 1877 but the family continued to run the mill until 1910 when it was sold to a syndicate. In 1924 it was bought by Portals of Laverstoke and was taken over by the Wiggins, Teape group in 1930.

The firm, now Arjo Wiggins Fine Papers Ltd., currently employs 150 people and produces 180 tonnes of paper per week, mainly government and commercial security papers, together with cotton content business stationery. In some of the work very accurate watermarking is required. Hand-cutting for this purpose was continued here until fairly recently, the mill being one of the last in the world where the process was thus performed, but the job of cutting to register for watermark position is now done mechanically, to the same high accuracy.

Most of the structure of the original mill has now disappeared, the main office block and a house near the present mill apparently being the only remains. The present impressive main factory building dates from 1862.

THE POWDER MILLS

During the latter half of the nineteenth century gunpowder was manufactured at a place still known as Powder Mills, beside the Cherry Brook, north-west of the B3212 road, about midway between Two Bridges and Postbridge (at SX 627774, etc; plates, pp. 161–2). The middle of Dartmoor may at first seem an odd place for a gunpowder factory, but then such factories have usually sought some measure of isolation for safety reasons. Land here was easily available, as were water power, building stone, and unlimited space to enable the various processing buildings to be dispersed, reducing the danger of spreading fire and explosions from one department to the next.

The pioneer of the Powder Mills was Mr George Frean, a Plymouth alderman, who started the industry in 1844. He rented this property, as he did other land on the moor, from the Duchy of Cornwall—which is still the landlord. Frean did much for the good of the moor and the people who lived on it, for many of whom conditions were then very hard, and being a man of enterprise, he sunk large sums of money in improving and developing Crown property on Dartmoor; he was complimented for his work by the Prince Consort. Later the work was carried on by Mr C. F. Williams, who was also highly regarded locally, until the mills closed down at the end of the century.

Our knowledge of the Dartmoor Powder Mills has recently been considerably widened by an archaeological survey undertaken in the summer of 1989 by Exeter Museum's Archaeological Field Unit, and presented in a report by Andrew Pye and Rosemary Robinson.

Gunpowder, or black powder as the Darmoor product is usually termed, was produced by combining a mixture of saltpetre (potassium nitrate), sulphur and charcoal. The process involved refinement of imported saltpetre by boiling and crystallization; grinding of all three constituents; mixing them in correct proportions; incorporation by crushing, mixing and churning; pressing the product into a 'cake', followed by breaking or granulation; and finally glazing, drying and finishing. Water, for processing and power, was brought by leats from the Cherry Brook and the East Dart.

On the hillside east of the Cherry Brook are the remains of three large rectangular mill buildings which are believed to have been used for the incorporation process. Their walls, of thickness and solidarity which have defied even moorland weather, show sheer vertical sides truly in plumb. Building them can have been no light task, with huge

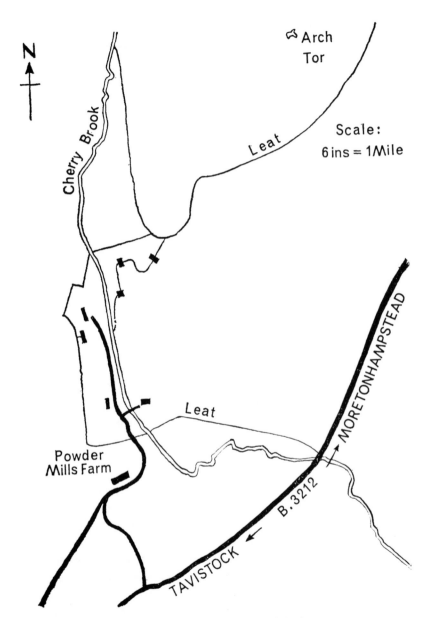

The Powder Mills buildings and part of the leat system

blocks of granite to be raised into position, many of them 6 ft long, 18 in high and of considerable thickness. The roofs of these buildings are long since gone: they were of deliberately light construction, of wood and tar, and could be blown off by an inadvertant explosion. Each building is divided into three. The middle section in each case contained an overshot waterwheel, with the leat passing through from one building to the next. It appears likely that each building contained on its upper floor an underdriven edge runner-mill. The mill-stones, not of granite, have been removed from the houses, and it appears that some of them, in sections, have been used for paving buildings on the west side of the brook.

The other buildings on the site include several smaller ones west of the Cherry Brook, which had walls of less robust construction which have been depleted for their stone over the years. Former roof timbers are said to have been used for firewood by American soldiers who were encamped here in large numbers during the second world war, and the troops are also believed to have been responsible for breaking the corners and edge off a limestone table in one of these buildings. It has been suggested that the gunpowder cake after incorporation was broken up on this table by means of wooden hammers, although machinery may also have been employed.

The chimney stacks still stand indomitable. They were necessary for taking fumes well away from the buildings, to which they were connected by flues, as any sparks were a danger. The precise purpose of the east-bank chimney is unclear, although possibly it was to do with charcoal production. The western chimney probably discharged fumes from a steam stove with central boiler which fed a system of pipes in a nearby long building where the powder, in final stages of production, was dried.

After undergoing finishing treatments the powder was tested and the method employed the use of a small mortar or éprouvette, still to be seen near the lane from the road where it has recently been remounted by the Duchy of Cornwall. An iron ball weighing about 68 lb was fired out of this, and the gunpowder could be graded according to the distance the ball travelled. Proving-mortars of the same type are believed to exist at a few other places in England, including Birmingham, Ambleside and Liphook.

Of remaining buildings at Powder Mills, a very few have been renovated and are now let by the Duchy of Cornwall for dwellings and small workshop industries. The land is let for livestock grazing. Several more cottages formerly existed to accommodate many of the workmen and their families. At times the mills employed a hundred men, some of whom came from as far afield as Chagford, Peter Tavy and Tavistock. Undoubtedly the employment provided was welcome to local people, especially with the decline of the tin industry. Although the Vitifer and Golden Dagger Mines, not far away, were still then functioning, often the work there was intermittent, and many who worked there at times would find casual work at Powder Mills, perhaps stacking barrels or cleaning out the leat, when tin-mining was at a standstill. There was a chapel here, too, a recognized Methodist preaching place, which many of the workers attended. Another building, situated nearby, was formerly a school, while a further one was originally the old cooper's house.

In the cooperage were made all the barrels in which the powder was sent away, and in addition all carpentry and repairs were done on the premises, involving their own section of the labour force. An old wheel-binding stone, on which cartwheels were placed during the fixing of the metal bands around their circumferences, is to be seen lying near the proving-mortar.

Great care had to be taken in all sorts of ways by those working on the premises to avoid explosions. One precaution was the regulation that the men had to leave their nailed boots behind when coming through the gate to the working area, in which, with so much explosive dust lying around on the stone floors, only soft shoes were permitted. A story is told of one worker here called Silas Sleep, who, apparently very conscious of the constant danger under which he laboured, used to eat his lunch and dinner together—just in case he perished in the forenoon.

The barrels of powder were dispatched from the mills on carts and wagons. Many were taken to Foggintor Quarries and stored there before being put on the railway for Plymouth. Most of the powder produced was used in the quarrying industry, a good deal being sent to Cornwall for the slate quarries. Some was probably used in road-making and a small quantity may have been bought by the mines working at the time. It was also used by moorland farmers for blasting away stone to clear ground for agriculture.

It was the invention of dynamite by Dr Alfred Nobel in the latter part of the nineteenth century which finally brought about the decrease in the demand for gunpowder and the end of the industry here on Dartmoor. Work ceased a little before 1900, never to start again. Left behind were some of the remains of the heaps of 'brimstone' and charcoal, fragments of which can still be seen, although much of the charcoal was afterwards fetched by local people and used for fuel. A small plantation of alder trees near the derelict buildings is a reminder that alderwood was considered the best for making the particular kind of charcoal needed.

AN ICEWORKS

On the north-western edge of Dartmoor, close to the craggy peaks of Sourton Tors, there existed during the nineteenth century an ice-making works. Increasing population created a growing demand for ice for food preservation, particularly for placing in the 'pads' of fish during transit by railway. Before mechanical means of refrigeration were developed natural methods of obtaining the ice had to be relied on.

The combination of a copious spring of clear water and temperatures which cause Sourton Tors to be snow-covered at least half a dozen times in almost any winter made the situation a suitable one both for preparing the ice and, more critical, for its storage until the hot summer months. Not a great deal is known about this minor industry, which appears to have had a short life: thought to have been established around 1875 it ceased in the 1880s.

The site of the iceworks, SX 546901, is nearly a mile up a very rough track from Sourton village, leading off the main Tavistock–Okehampton road (A386) near Sourton Church and ascending close beneath the tors and around to the north of them. The works lay at an altitude of between 1,300 and 1,400 ft above sea level, in a slight dip before the land slopes up again towards Corn Ridge. The herbage is grassy, and undulations mark the remains of shallow pits or ponds in which the ice was formed and stored.

A Mr Henderson, C.E., of Truro (probably the later founder of a mining school in Truro), writing in the *Mining Journal* (12 February 1876)[1] described the works as comprising thirty ponds, giving a 'chessboard' appearance on the hillside. This evidently squarish ponds were said to be 3 ft in depth, brick-sided, cement-lined and turfed to the edges. After water run into the ponds had frozen, the ice was cut out in blocks and stored in a nearby building capable of taking several hundred tons. Doubtless this building would have been insulated with earth and turf. In spring and early summer the ice was carted downhill in wagons and probably transported to Plymouth and elsewhere on the recently established London & South Western Railway.

The water came from a spring a few yards up the hillside—a clear spring issuing from one place, surrounded by comparatively dry ground, free of rushes. This was reputedly a never-failing supply, and during the winter it was conveyed in pipes to the works just below. Several of the pipes and broken pieces have come to light over the years. The daughter of a former employee described in her later years how she remembered, when taking up her father's midday pasty meal on a hot summer's day, that the sudden cold on approaching the entrance to the store would seem to 'take the breath away'. In a cool season the supply of stored ice apparently sometimes lasted until July, but once removed fron insulation liquefaction soon set in. No doubt the time taken in transit meant that considerable wastage of the ice occurred before it reached its destination and such losses probably accounted for the industry's short duration.

After the closure of the iceworks and until the second world war

[1] I am grateful to Mr Justin Brooke for drawing my attention to this piece of information.

there was little to be seen at ground level, save the undulations. Then American military forces, during exercises, dug 'fox-holes' here and the covered building remains were opened up. Since their exposure much of the stone used in the construction, which originally came from a quarry nearby, has been removed and used for building purposes elsewhere.

A GLASS FACTORY

In Okehampton parish, east of the hamlet of Meldon, and on the opposite side of the West Okement River and the main railway line (at SX 566922), are the site and a few remains of a former glassworks, close to the now disused granulite (aplite) quarry. This vein of mineral was discovered in the 1880s and amongst other uses was for some time successfully employed in glass-making, the granulite being of high quality and, containing potash, soda and alumina, having nearly sufficient alkali to melt the silica of which it is principally composed.

In about 1885 the quarry was leased by a Mr Charles Green who subsequently arranged with a syndicate to undertake its working and that of the lime quarries nearby. Bottles were made from a formula of granulite (calcined) 700 parts, marble (uncalcined) 150 parts, carbonate of soda 75 parts, manganese 45 parts, the glass being easily worked. The latest spell of activity in this industry is said to have been for about eighteen months around 1920, when Dutch and German glass-blowers were employed. Light-green glass mineral and medicine bottles were made, but apparently there was difficulty in getting the glass sufficiently clear.

The site can be reached by taking a small turning opposite a café about 2 miles from Okehampton to the south of the Okehampton–Launceston road, continuing on the lane for nearly a mile, and going under the viaduct. Near the quarry cottages a road leads off to the granulite quarry on the right-hand side. The glassworks was near this, close to the entrance, but all that can be seen are some rubble from the buildings and broken remains of the green bottles.

A CANDLE FACTORY

At Sticklepath, on the north side of the main street there was in the early nineteenth century a small candle-making works, associated with Chandler's Cottage by the entrance to the Devonshire Inn. Both at Manor Mills and at Western or Carnalls Mills in the village, bones were ground at that time, and the tallow from the bones was used for the candles and rush-dips. The pith for the wicks was obtained from rushes gathered in a nearby meadow.

WATER EXTRACTION FOR DOMESTIC NEEDS

With the growth of towns, neighbouring public authorities have long looked covetously at Dartmoor's clear and plentiful water, with its gravitational advantage. The earliest to do so was the Corporation of Plymouth, local sources of water in the sixteenth century proving inadequate for the demands of the increasing population and the large fleets of ships in the port. In 1584, during the reign of Elizabeth I, Sir Francis Drake was a member of a Select Committee which approved a Bill for bringing water from the River Meavy to Plymouth, as the town's first public supply. Following this, in 1585, an Act of Parliament authorized its construction, and the leat was made between December 1590 and April 1591. Seventeen miles in length and about 6 ft wide and 2 ft deep, it was without its present solid floor and granite sides for at least a century.

The intake of the Plymouth leat was on the site of the present Burrator reservoir, and for some of its way over the rocky ground it was carried in large wooden launders. The leat ran west, looping around Yennadon, to Roborough Down and across the area now covered by the village of Yelverton. Following a roughly southward course across the Down it continued towards Plymouth, passing over present-day Crownhill. For part of its way the course of the leat is still clearly traceable, especially on Roborough Down, though much of its route, particularly at Yelverton and in the environs of Plymouth, is within private grounds. There is a legend, not necessarily apocryphal, that at its inauguration Drake rode on a white horse ahead of the initial flow of water, leading it all the way to Plymouth.

For 300 years the leat continued as Plymouth's supply. During the nineteenth century a number of small service reservoirs were constructed on the town outskirts, the last of which was the Roborough

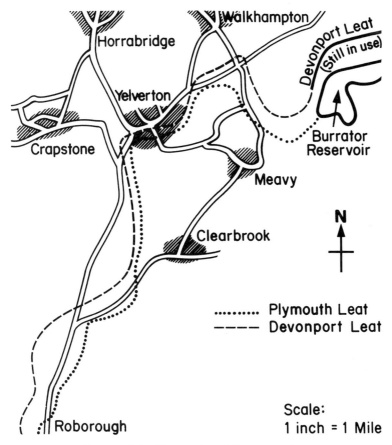

Routes of the Plymouth and Devonport leats

reservoir completed in 1885, and after this date the southern portion of the leat was abandoned and the supply from here piped. The northern section, about 8 miles in length, remained in use until, at the end of the nineteenth century, the Burrator reservoir was constructed, fed from the same source—the River Meavy. When completed in September 1898 the area covered by water totalled 116 acres. In 1928 the dam was heightened and a further 34 acres flooded.

The Devonport leat is another which augments Plymouth Corporation's supply, having been inaugurated as a result of the powers obtained in 1793 by the company of Proprietors of the Plymouth Dock Waterworks. The leat takes water from the West Dart, the Cowsic and the Blackbrook in the area north of Princetown, and passes east of the village to the Whiteworks vicinity on its winding way to its destination. Among its interesting features the leat has a number of aqueducts, flows through a 648-yd tunnel near Nun's Cross and forms a moderately spectacular waterfall as it descends the western slopes of Raddick Hill into the valley of the River Meavy, which it crosses by an iron launder (plate, p. 198). Formerly the supply continued from here to Dousland and over Roborough Down via Crownhill to Devonport, but it is now diverted to enter Burrator reservoir.

Since these early undertakings were constructed the greater part of Devon has come to draw its water supplies from Dartmoor, and reservoirs have multiplied. These themselves are obviously far from being archaeology, though some conceal features which are. The remains of a tinners' blowing-house lie beneath the waters of Burrator reservoir; another, as well as the old course of the moorland road, is submerged beneath Venford reservoir on Holne Moor, constructed prior to 1907. The Avon reservoir, completed in 1959, covers fifty acres of Dean and Brent Moors, a valley much worked by early tinners, and also conceals a blowing house.

The owners of individual moorland farmsteads have also, of course, helped themselves to water. Where neither a stream nor a spring was within immediate reach of the desired site, a more distant brook might be tapped and a leat constructed. Some of the old warren houses employed this means, Ditsworthy being a good example, the leat in this case passing through the house itself. Often these 'pot-water' leats served more than one house or farm. A 'bull's-eye', a hole of about 1–1½ in diameter in a block of stone built into the side of the leat, was commonly used at the point of extraction. Bull's-eyes, or 'inch-holes' can be seen where water is extracted from the Grimstone and Sortridge leat at points on Whitchurch Common between the granite cross known as Windy Post (SX 535744), north of Feather Tor, and Plaster Down.

HYDRO-ELECTRICITY

Electrical pioneers saw the potential value of the momentum of Dartmoor water in the later years of the nineteenth century, and before its end there were at least two commercial undertakings on the edge of the moor generating hydro-electricity and supplying customers with power for lighting.

The first of these was at Okehampton, where water from the East Okement was used by Mr Henry Geen, a builder and timber-merchant, and founder of the firm of Blatchford, Ash & Co, to power a turbine operating a 110-volt dynamo for working machinery in his timber-yard. The venture was so successful that before long, in 1888, it was extended for lighting purposes to nearby houses and other buildings. The demand continued to increase and soon, and at successive stages, additional and more advanced plant was installed. Eventually, in 1930, the West Devon Electricity Supply Company took over. There are now no signs of this early electrical venture at Okehampton, its site being the property of the South Western Electricity Board.

Chagford followed close behind Okehampton in being amongst the first towns in the whole country to receive the benefits of electric lighting. (Reference to this was made on p. 120.) The pioneer at Chagford was Mr G. H. Reed, who adapted the 14-ft diameter ×

14-ft breast undershot waterwheel of his mill to work a lighting plant operating at 2,000 volts, first illuminating the town on 1 September 1891. The water for this came from the River Teign by a leat. Again various changes in the machinery subsequently took place, including the removal of the old wheel in 1914 and its replacement with the present turbine, and, like that at Okehampton, the Chagford undertaking was amalgamated into the West Devon Electricity Supply Co in 1930. Hydro-electricity is still generated on the same site at Chagford though in a newer building, now under the Central Electricity Generating Board, and fed into the national grid. The former building has been demolished.

Much later in the field was the hydro-electric venture at Mary Tavy, now very much in active production, and though small having the distinction of being the biggest hydro-electric station in England. The River Tavy supplies most of the water, much of it being brought along the Reddaford leat, described in the Gazetteer (p. 213). As already mentioned, this leat had previously served the important mines in this vicinity. Mining declined towards the end of the nineteenth century and in 1891 the Manor of Mary Tavy, the property of the Buller family, was sold, including the water rights of the leat. The catalogue of the sale shows that these water rights had been granted to John Buller in 1824, probably about twenty or so years after the leat's construction. At the sale the water rights of the leat were bought by a Tavistock foundry owner, but later changed hands a number of times between various mining firms. In 1932 the water rights were acquired by the West Devon Mining & Power Company, incorporated in the West Devon Electricity Supply Co. Mr F. Christie was a leading light of this firm, which had already taken over the undertakings at Okehampton, Chagford and elsewhere, its object being to amalgamate a number of small concerns into one comprehensive scheme for the production of electricity. Mr Christie saw the obvious advantages of the 70-in annual rainfall in the watershed of the fast-flowing River Tavy, and of the ready-made leat.

The initial development of the Mary Tavy hydro-electric system made use of power from water taken from the Tavy at points other than that of the intake of the Reddaford leat. The first of these involved the construction of a mile-long channel, with a 100-yd tunnel, to bring water to Mary Tavy from Hillbridge, while for the second phase another power station was built some distance away, at Morwellham beside the River Tamar, and fed by water from the old Tavistock Canal, taking water from the Tavy at the Abbey Weir in Tavistock. In 1936 it was decided to develop the Reddaford supply as a third and largest source.

In that year work began on reconditioning the old leat, and building a curved reservoir beside the old workings at Wheal Jewell on Black Down to hold 6,000,000 gallons of water. A screen house and a valve house were also built, and 2 miles of 3 ft 6 in diameter piping laid to carry the water down the fall of 560 ft to the generators at Mary Tavy—built on the site of the old South Friendship mine. A very wet season prolonged the work and delayed completion, but the scheme was put into operation in August 1937. After use, the water is returned to the Tavy just below the power station.

In 1948 the system was nationalized, and was then run by the Central Electricity Generating Board, the electricity produced supplementing the national grid. The Board took over the West Devon Mining & Power Co as a small subsidiary on nationalization, in order to retain the water rights, and thus acquired also the mining rights and the title of Lord of the Manor of Mary Tavy. The power station is now run by National Power Plc.

In addition to these public undertakings a number of smaller hydro-electric schemes have been set up for private premises, usually making use of the old leats of former mills. The particularly enterprising scheme of the Perryman family at Yeo Mills, Chagford, is described in the Gazetteer.

CHAPTER SEVEN

Agriculture and Kindred Pursuits

AGRICULTURE has been a means of livelihood as well as a primary way of life on Dartmoor ever since man first settled there centuries ago. Its pursuit has never been easy. Even if climatic conditions were less harsh in prehistoric times the shallow, acid soil cannot have been more fertile then than now. Its cultivation through the ages has been a struggle against the elements—geological, physical and climatic; for a while man and his efforts might seem to win, but time and again natural conditions would gain the better of him and he would be forced to withdraw, perhaps to seek an easier living on the lowlands. The sites of agricultural enterprise and toil thus became abandoned, though perhaps only to await further attempts at cultivation by others at a later stage.

EARLY FARMING

But though agricultural traditions, like early civilizations, have come and gone, they have left their marks upon the scene. Increasing light on former farming practices has been shed by observations and investigations made in recent years, and it is probable that as yet uncovered evidence remains, which could further piece together the agricultural history of the moor. Many abandoned sites are of ancient origin, though not all; that present farming on the moor differs widely from that practised 200 or even 100 years ago is amply recorded, whether by derelict isolated farmsteads or by signs of former ploughing and cultivation, now reverted to moorland sward.

The earliest known Dartmoor agriculturalists were the people of the Bronze Age. They kept sheep and cattle, and the pounds or enclosures which they have left behind, such as the one at Grimspound,

(left) *The 45 ft pitchback waterwheel opposite Dry Lake at Henroost Mine, Hexworthy, c 1918. It was removed c 1934;* (right) *The same scene in 1986. The large wheelpit has been shored up by the Dartmoor National Park Authority*

Page 144 (above) *Belford Mill, Ashburton, which has in its day served as both woollen mill and corn mill; sometimes nicknamed Coffin Mill on account of its unusual shape;* (below) *From an advertisement of Hamlyn Brothers Ltd, c 1910 : the layout of the woollen mills at Buckfastleigh, seen from the north side. Reduced now by demolition*

were built as much for the safe protection and control of stock as for containing together the hut dwellings: human enemies, as well as wolves, had to be fended off. These people also cultivated the soil, though at least the earlier generations would not have known the plough, using stout sticks in their attempts at getting a suitable tilth.

More is becoming known about the farming systems of the moor dwellers of the second millenium BC from recent research concerning reaves—low, vegetation-covered walls which extend over moorland, sometimes for a few miles. Aerial photography has greatly complemented literary and field study in advancing the research. Study of the reaves was pioneered in the 1960s by John Somers Cocks and by Elizabeth Gawne, and further developed by Andrew Fleming.

The groupings of reaves appear to indicate the territorial arrangements of the Bronze Age communities, each having its own area of grazing land (often subdivided) in the lower area near the settlement enclosures, and also a section marked by parallel reaves used partly for cultivation. In addition, probably slightly later contours provided a boundary against the higher level grazing land. The prehistoric reaves, some of which may have been taller than now, usually differ from later banks which are more often of earth rather than stone, with ditches. Reave systems have been observed in the valleys of the Upper Dart, Plym, Meavy, Yealm, Erme, Avon, and North and South Teign, and on Whitchurch Common, Rippon Tor, Shapley Common, Cosdon and Meldon.

The apparent abandonment of the moor by farmers for a period from around 500 BC is attributed to changes towards a more severe climate that developed from that time. The high moorland was probably uninhabited for several centuries, although some Celtic presence appears likely. Settlement of Devon by the Saxons began from the seventh century, but apart from lower slopes the greater part of Dartmoor remained unfarmed into medieval times. Cultivations gradually crept up around the edges, however, and by 1086 had reached the 900 ft contour on the western side and the 1,200 level on the east. In some cases the small square or rectangular fields of earlier cultivators, bounded by banks or by stones set on edge, such as occur on Horridge Common (Ilsington) and on Rippon Tor, were adapted by medieval farmers. Babeny, on the Walla Brook, and Pizwell were recorded as hamlets in 1260, so had by that date probably existed for some time. Each has now only a single farmstead. Probably becoming established, too, at about this time were the later-abandoned medieval settlements, some of which have in recent years been investigated and excavated.

One of these is on the slopes of Hound Tor, in Manaton parish, where excavations were begun in 1961 under the late Mrs M. Minter (plate, p. 180). In this case the stone-built medieval houses of which remnants have been found were constructed on the site of earlier turf ones dated from the tenth or eleventh century or rather later. The village consisted of three barns and eight long rectangular houses, these each being divided into two, one half being for dwelling in and the other for winter accommodation of animals. The barns contained kilns in which it is thought the corn would have been dried over burning straw. Around the Hound Tor village is evidence of 60 acres of cultivated fields.

Other deserted sites have been recently investigated by Mrs C. D. Linehan, who recorded a number of them in the *Transactions of the Devonshire Association*, Vol XCVII. Sites have been found in parishes all over the moor and invariably seem to have been connected with an agricultural way of life. Previous research work carried out on abandoned sites in Widecombe-in-the-Moor parish by Mrs Linehan and Mr Hermon French is recorded in an earlier volume of *Transactions of the Devonshire Association*, Vol XCV. At the abandoned village of Blackaton (SX 698783), close to the road from Moretonhampstead to Widecombe, which passes through the site, have been found the remains of a number of 'long'-houses of the type already mentioned, surrounded by an extensive area of early field systems marked by faint plough ridges. Much of this evidence has, however, now been obliterated by a bulldozer.

Generally it does not seem that the open-field system was common on Dartmoor, collections of small, irregularly-shaped fields farmed by individuals appearing more usual from the evidence surrounding the sites of medieval farmsteads. There may be some exceptions, however, as for example in places on slopes above the valley of the West Webburn, where fairly conspicuous field systems can be observed contouring the hillsides, particularly in the vicinity of Challacombe. There is evidence here of certain ploughing, which, on the sloping ground, has produced banks or lynchets in a very pronounced form. Photographs have revealed how the ends of these are staggered, presumably to allow the plough to be taken up for work on the higher slopes (plate, p. 180). Many of the farms scratched from the open moor in medieval times date from between 1150 and 1250. At this stage settlement was mainly only on the edges of the moor, and surface stone was used for constructing the house and other buildings and for the boundary walls. Cholwich Town, in Cornwood parish, and Brisworthy, Meavy, are examples of farmsteads founded at this period.

Eventually the pioneers advanced further into the moor, and carved out farms for themselves in its more sheltered and verdant spots. So arose in the thirteenth and fourteenth centuries those farms known as the 'ancient tenements', of which at one time there were thirty-five, all lying within the area of the royal Forest. Some were grouped three or more in one place, as at Brimpts, Dunnabridge and Huccaby, while others, like Dury, Hartland and Prince Hall, were isolated. The farmers concerned were tenants because they held the tenements by 'Copy of Court Roll' from the lord of the manor—the Duchy—but they were to all intents freeholders, though not in the way understood today. Certain duties were required of the holders or the tenements, in the form of attending the courts at Lydford Castle, and assisting at the annual drifts of sheep and cattle to Dunnabridge Pound or Creber Pound, but in return they had the rights of grazing, turf-cutting (turbary) and stone-taking in the Forest, and also, until 1796, of enclosing an 8-acre 'newtake' if three generations of one family had held the farm consecutively.

The name 'Forest' does not necessarily, in the case of Dartmoor, denote an area covered with trees, but signifies its reservation as a royal hunting ground, subject to Forest Law, after the rest of Devon was disafforested in the reign of King John. The boundary of the Forest follows that of the parish of Lydford, all of which lies within its bounds except for a small portion on the west. Surrounding the Forest are twenty-six border parishes, twenty-two of which actually touch its boundary. Within the ring of parishes the moorland area constitutes the Commons of Devon, claimed as a 'parcel of the Duchy of Cornwall' since its creation and, like the Forest, administered by the Lord of the Manor of Lydford. Ownership of the Commons is now settled under the Commons Registration Act.

Certain owners and occupiers of land in the parishes surrounding the moor had, on payment of 'venville' rents (a corruption of the term 'fin ville'), certain rights within the Forest as well as on the Commons, and were known as venville tenants. These rights consisted of grazing and the taking of 'coals', turf, heath, furze and stones. Like the holders of the ancient tenements, they were obliged to attend the Lydford courts and to assist at the drifts. Originally the rights of pasturage applied only to the hours of daylight, but this was extended to permit stock to remain overnight on the annual payment of a small fee. A man was not permitted to pasture more stock in the Forest than he could winter on his farm. It is interesting to note that even the other people of Devon, with the exception of the inhabitants of Totnes and Barnstaple, had certain grazing rights on the Commons.

Dartmoor farmhouses were from very early times built of granite. Because of its long-lasting qualities and the fact that fresh supplies were freely available, an older building would often be allowed to remain, generally to be used for housing livestock, when a better house was built. At Cholwich Town, Cornwood, for instance, as well as the Tudor farmhouse dating from the early sixteenth century there are the remains of an older previous building with thick granite walls, probably built in the thirteenth. There are a number of similar later examples. At Cudlipptown, Peter Tavy, an early sixteenth-century dwelling near the present farmhouse is now used as one of the farm buildings. At Yeo, Chagford, a fifteenth-century building is now a barn, while another, even older, is used for stock; in both of these former dwellings fireplaces can still be seen.

Most Dartmoor medieval farmhouses were built on the 'long-house' principle, the fairly standard arrangement being for living quarters to be at one end, with accommodation for cattle, and at times probably sheep and horses too, at the other. The same thatched roof covered both parts, with a central entrance-passage used by all. Eventually the stock were ousted to other buildings elsewhere, and their previous quarters incorporated into the dwelling house. The general arrangement, with the central passage, was still retained. There is at least one instance on Dartmoor where until modern times the passage was a right of way for the general public using a footpath from the moorland fringe to the local village church. At Youlditch Farm, Peter Tavy, a similar passage was thus used as late as the nineteenth century. (The right of way registered under present legislation takes a deviating route west of the farm.)

There are very many examples of long-houses throughout the moorland parishes, used as dwellings still, and such farmhouses are quite easily recognizable. Shilston, Throwleigh is a particularly good example.

A number of farms, particularly on the eastern side of Dartmoor, possessed ash houses, situated a short distance from the farmhouse, often close beside the road. Here ashes from the domestic fires were stored until required as a fertilizer on the land. The buildings are described by R. Hansford Worth (*Dartmoor*, pp. 415 and 416), who mentions examples of conical ones at Lower Hisley, Lustleigh, and at Shapley and West Combe, North Bovey (plate, p. 182). There are also some rectangular ones, for example at Frenchbeer, Chagford, and Way, Lustleigh.

The beginning of the Black Death, in 1349, caused a halt in the establishment of new farms, and even in some cases abandonment of settlements. For the next 200 years very little change took place, but in the sixteenth and seventeenth centuries some of the existing farms were enlarged and even some new ones created out of the waste, the practice being to plough and crop these for three or four successive seasons. Such expansion continued for some years.

CROPS AND METHODS

There is no doubt that arable farming was practised on the moor from an early date. Apart from the evidence of the early tilling fields already described, the fact that the mill at Babeny was established before 1303 clearly indicates that corn was grown at that time. Rye straw found in the thatch of old buildings suggests that rye was perhaps the commonest cereal crop. Later, in the seventeenth century, the land around Babeny was described as 'good', suggesting crops of oats and rye, and even, with special manuring, barley also.

It is reputed that potatoes were grown on Dartmoor during the Napoleonic Wars and it is considered by Mr Somers Cocks that it was to the cultivation of these, as well as of corn, that the more recent of the well-defined ridge-and-furrow systems owe their origin. A good example of this one-time cultivation can be seen above Culley Combe, close to the junction of the Postbridge–Moretonhampstead road (B3212) with the road leading south to Widecombe. This late eighteenth or early nineteenth-century work would have been done by ox-drawn ploughs, producing broad ridges about $7\frac{1}{2}$ ft across, and ploughing appears frequently to have been done up and down the slope rather than along it, probably to aid drainage in this area of high rainfall.

Another early relic of the growing of potatoes are the storage caves on some Dartmoor farms within the granite area. Cut into the side of sloping ground at a point convenient to the farmhouse, these tunnels were perhaps up to 40 ft in length, about 6 ft high and of similar or slightly narrower breadth. The entrance would be fitted with a wooden door. A description of such structures is given in *Dartmoor* by Worth, who also quotes examples of farms where they have been observed, including Colly Town, Leather Tor, Deancombe and Routrundle (see plate on p. 159).

Even well into the nineteenth century, methods and equipment employed in Dartmoor farming remained primitive. Wheeled vehicles were still little used for agricultural purposes, transport of materials of all kinds being performed by pack-horses or donkeys fitted either with panniers or with crooks. Panniers were commonly used for carrying peat, while dung-pots for taking manure out to the fields were carried by the same means. Crooks were formed from a pair of 10-ft poles, bent into shape while green and connected by horizontal bars. These were slung over the pack saddle and would be used for carrying sheaves of corn, faggots of wood, furze and bracken for bedding. Shorter, stouter crooks, known as crubs, would be used for carrying heavier things like logs. The goods the farmer took to market for sale, which included potatoes, poultry, eggs, scalded cream and butter, were invariably carried in panniers, usually on the backs of donkeys.

Before the cart came into general use sledges were widely used on the farms for carrying bigger loads, often of heavy stones, and were particularly in evidence at harvest times. Oxen were used for draught purposes and for ploughing, while the use of the flail or threshel for threshing the corn continued in some cases up to the century's end. This laborious task was performed by two men who, facing each other, threshed the corn with alternating strokes of their flails for hours on end, day after day.

THE 'IMPROVERS'

The system by which the holder of an ancient tenement could enclose a newtake of up to 8 acres if his father and grandfather had been in continuous occupation before him ceased in 1796. The privilege had, in any case, never been exploited to its full extent. But at the end of the eighteenth century, and into the nineteenth, newtakes of a different and far more extensive kind began to bite into the moor.

Fired with the enthusiasm characteristic of that age there came a succession of 'improvers', some of them learned gentlemen, whose conscientious plan it was to 'develop' Dartmoor and change it from being a barren wilderness to an area of agricultural fertility and prosperity. The enclosing of large newtakes went on at this time, under grant from the Duchy and supported by an Act of Parliament of 1822, in a fashion altogether contrary to former Forest practice.

One of the earliest of these optimistic pioneers was a Mr Gullett who enclosed land at Prince Hall and constructed farm buildings there on the site of the ancient tenement. Meanwhile, a Tavistock solicitor, Mr Edward Bray, the Duke of Bedford's steward, started reclaiming land at Bear Down. Soon also upon the scene was Mr (later Sir) Thomas Tyrwhitt, a man equally well known for his other non-agricultural Dartmoor projects, and Lord Warden of the Stannaries. Tyrwhitt's aim was 'to reclaim and clothe with grain and grasses a spacious tract of land, now lying barren, desolate and neglected, to fill this unoccupied region with an industrious and hardy population'. In 1785 he set to work in establishing the place he later named Tor Royal, $\frac{1}{2}$ mile south-east of Princetown, expending large sums of money in various schemes of improvement, draining, ploughing and laying down to grass.

Other men were responsible for further enclosing, cultivation and planting at around this time, resulting in the numerous areas bounded with stone walls commonly seen today, particularly in the vicinity of Two Bridges and Postbridge. Prince Hall was later bought from Gullett by Mr Justice Buller, who continued its development, and in 1846 by a Mr G. W. Fowler, who lavished vast sums of money upon the place and succeeded in raising some excellent crops, including enormous turnips for which he became locally famous. Eventually he came to the conclusion that corn-growing and the uncertainties of harvesting in this situation did not warrant the expense, and the land was laid down to grass. It was Fowler's successor, a Mr Lamb, who introduced the Scottish sheep and cattle on Dartmoor. The farm attached to the prison was also started as a pioneering enterprise in the nineteenth century. Great reclamation was done here in the latter half of the century by the use of convict labour, and the land divided into fields separated by walls made of granite brought from the prison quarries.

After fortunes had disappeared and unceasing toil had reaped scant reward, even those most anxious to help the local population and most convinced of the efficacy of the newer agricultural methods, were forced to admit that cultivation of the moor was generally an impracticable proposition. In addition, as the 'improvers' had appropriated the best and potentially the most fertile parts of the moor, opposition was coming both from those by now concerned with the preservation of the wildness of Dartmoor and from the Commoners, who, as they rapidly lost the more choice parts of their grazing, felt that their rights were being interfered with. Finally a stop was put to further encroachments, though not before 15,000 acres of Dartmoor had been enclosed during the years between 1820 and the end of the century.

The granite walls in this central part of Dartmoor, around the intersection of the two main roads which cross it, are a constant reminder of the agricultural efforts over nearly the last two centuries. These walls, of 4 to 5 ft in height, are without mortar or turf filling, and have bigger spaces between the stones than have some of the dry-stone walls traditional in other parts of the country. The early ones are of undressed stone, though in the later stages larger and roughly squared stone was used. The building of the newtake walls was a recognized occupation on the moor in the early days of the nineteenth century, but one which died, or became restricted to dividing existing enclosures or repair work, as the enclosing of fresh land ceased.

It was not only the more spectacular 'improvers' who tried their fortunes on the land of Dartmoor in the nineteenth century. Countless smaller and more modest ventures were started. It was in this way that, for instance, the collection of small farms at Peat Cot, south of Princetown, grew up, as well as numerous others. As the hard truth that Dartmoor was not made for arable agriculture eventually dawned, the farmers had to cut their losses and leave, or stick to grass and stock. Ruined farmsteads in various parts of the moor tell the tale of such abandoned enterprises. Fox Tor Farm, built early in the nineteenth century, has long been in ruins, and remote Teignhead Farm, built in 1808 by a Mr Rogers and occupied subsequently by a succession of farmers, has lain deserted a number of years. Nun's Cross Farm was started at a rather later date, but the dwellings there, too, are now abandoned (see p. 204 and plate on p. 197). A number of now-ruined farmsteads in the area of the River Meavy and the Narrator Brook were abandoned in the 1890s when Burrator Reservoir was being constructed and the whole catchment area had to be cleared, though some of the houses had already been deserted and their land amalgamated with other farms.

During the last years of the nineteenth century the greater part of the moor was used primarily as summer grazing ground rather than for all-the-year stocking. South-Devon-type store and dry cattle grazed it from May to October, belonging not only to those farmers holding enclosed land on the periphery, but also to many others from the lowland areas who sent cattle on some form of agistment, either legally through the Duchy of Cornwall tenants or perhaps illegally through farming friends who held Common rights. Sheepflocks of that time were mainly of the long-woolled Dartmoor breed, smaller and hardier than their modern counterparts; there were two kinds— Whiteface 'Widecombes' on the east and Dartmoor proper on the west and north. Ewes and lambs grazed in summer, 'leared' on the hills by wethers grazing for longer spells to produce wool and mutton. Today the Galloway cattle herds and Scotch Blackface ewe flocks, breeds first introduced in this region by Lamb of Prince Hall, are the predominating ones on the moor.

WARRENING

Through several centuries the warrening of rabbits was a feature of the Dartmoor scene and played its part in the economy of the area.

The term 'warren' originally denoted land set apart for the preservation of game—hare and rabbit, pheasant and partridge—under the Crown, but more recently on Dartmoor it described merely areas where the breeding of rabbits in the natural state was encouraged, followed by their killing and commercial use for food.

It is believed that rabbits were introduced into this country from the Continent by the Normans, and there is documentary evidence that they existed on Dartmoor in the twelfth century, the earliest of the warrens being those in the vicinity of the River Plym. Others were later set up in different parts of the moor. The practice continued here and there until almost the present time—until, following the myxomatosis epidemic of 1954, the final halt was called by rabbit-clearance legislation in 1955.

Where a warren was to be established it was the custom to set up long banks or 'buries' in which the rabbits could live and breed. A bury was made by first digging a trench with branches leading from it, bridged over with stones, and covered over with more stones and soil, leaving entrance holes. Once introduced upon the scene the rabbits would soon find these and make themselves at home, and the banks eventually grassed over to form the green buries still prominent on the warrens today. Drainage was important in order to prevent the buries becoming too damp or flooded, and for this reason they were often made on hillsides and were provided with surrounding ditches. Their length varied from 5 to over 80 yd, being usually around 30. In order to keep the rabbits as far as possible within the area use was made whenever practicable of rivers or streams as natural barriers, while in other places a wall was built.

A warren house where the warrener would live was usually provided, with nearby accommodation for the dogs, which were an important part of the system. In several cases, for example at Ditsworthy (SX 584663), the remains of these buildings can still be seen.

The rabbits were allowed to breed during the summer, and were caught in large numbers from September to March. The exact method adopted in the earliest days is not known, but in more recent times long nets were used. In the late evening, when the rabbits were feeding on the higher ground, these would be staked out across the area of the warren. Some hours later, around dawn, the men and the dogs would come and drive the rabbits into the nets, where they would be caught and killed. Loaded on to donkeys the rabbits would then be taken back to the warren house, paunched and dispatched to Plymouth and elsewhere. Those marketed at Plymouth would be skinned as they were sold, the skins being brought back, dried and later sold to furriers. Ferrets were also kept to assist in extracting rabbits from the more difficult places.

The warrener's constant enemies were vermin—stoats and weasels. Before the introduction of the shot gun, traps for catching them were devised out of stone: the remains of many of these are still in evidence on most of the warrens. Generally a large stone slab, perhaps 4 ft in length, was let into the ground, level with its surface, on top of which were laid three heavy dressed stones. The longest of these was laid along the length of the base stone, the other two being laid parallel to it, with a space between them. A passage was left between the long stone and the two short ones. Thus there would be three openings, one at each end, and one at the side between the two short side stones (diagram opposite and plate on p. 182). The side opening was permanently closed, usually by a slate sufficiently thin to enable a hole to be made in it through which the wire operating the tripping mechanism could pass. The whole was covered with a large flat stone having on its upper surface two holes. These were for holding posts supporting slates at each end which operated vertically through grooves provided on the insides of the side stones. When an animal entered and reached the centre it would trip off the wire through the side slate to the posts above, causing the slates at each end to drop, trapping it within.

The remains of over eighty vermin traps have been recorded on the moor; over sixty of them in the Plym valley, one of the best and almost complete examples being on Legis Tor. No bait was used in the traps, which were sited where vermin were known to have their habitual runs. Low 'funnel' walls directed them to the trap entrance. Often these were sited near earlier enclosure walls, sometimes built into them, and these would then play a part in the layout, the funnel walls being modified accordingly.

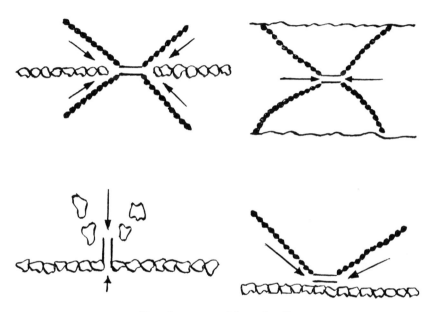

Vermin traps and funnel walls

The matter of vermin traps is dealt with at some length by R. Hansford Worth in *Dartmoor*. A more recent leading authority on the subject of Dartmoor warrens was the late R. G. Haynes, who conducted considerable research in this field. His detailed account of the warrens, together with plans and drawings of all known vermin traps, is deposited with Plymouth City Library, Local History section. Mr Haynes' investigations cover over a dozen areas of the moor, briefly described here in the Gazetteer. The main warrens were in the valley of the Plym, where there were five—Trowlesworthy, Willings

Walls and Hentor in Shaugh Prior parish, and Legis Tor and Ditsworthy in Sheepstor. There was another in Sheepstor parish, close to
the tor itself, and others at Headland (North Bovey), Huntingdon, in
the southern part of Lydford parish, Vaghill (Widecombe), Merrivale (Walkhampton), Wistman's (Lydford) and Skaigh (South
Tawton).

CHARCOAL BURNING

Charcoal burning was a fairly widespread practice in the border
woodlands of the moor, apparently continuing into the present
century. This late survival is evident from a photograph of a man
with a packhorse fitted with crooks near Fingle Bridge, reproduced in
A Dartmoor Century 1883–1983. Taken by Robert Burnard in 1905,
the original photograph included in its caption: 'these carry water
from the river to the charcoal burners in Hore Wood'. Mr Brian Le
Messurier reports finding charcoal burners' platforms in such woodlands, particularly on the east, notably in the Teign valley and that of
the Dart at Hembury. The platforms where the kilns were situated,
of similar size to Bronze Age hut circles, appear to have been dug out
of the hillsides particularly in areas where coppicing has been
regularly carried out.

The charcoal was produced by burning branch wood with
insufficient oxygen for complete combustion. This was achieved by
stacking the wood to a dome shape and covering with turf and earth.
Air was allowed to enter until the wood was fully alight, when inlets
were mostly blocked. The continuing heat then caused removal of
volatile substances with retention of carbon. After some days the
burning was stopped by completely blocking off the air supply and
allowing the charcoal to cool, often with the aid of water. The
charcoal was used for various chemical and metallurgical processes.

BARK STRIPPING

The bark of young deciduous trees, chiefly oak, was used for dyeing in the tanneries and much bark was stripped from the trees of the Dartmoor border valleys for this purpose. The work was known as 'ripping', and at times many men found in it a welcome chance of a job. The area of Dewerstone woods, by the rivers Plym and Meavy, was one of the places where this was done, and much of the oak still to be seen here and in other valleys was deliberately coppiced for this trade.

Other activities involving the harvesting of the moor's natural vegetation have at various times almost assumed the status of minor industries. These have included the collecting of lichens for dye of a different kind, the gathering of sedges for use in filling mattresses, and the summer picking of whortleberries for sale in the towns. By their nature, however, these 'industries' have left no visible remains.

Page 159   *Potato cave at the abandoned and ruined Leather Tor Farm, Walkhampton.*

CHAPTER EIGHT

Communications

THOUGH later than the rest of Devon in developing a road system, Dartmoor was no less known to the pack-horse traveller. Often a route over the moor was preferable to the deep and miry lanes of the lower surrounding country, and although lying over steep and exposed ground had at least the advantage of directness. Though much of Dartmoor is wet and boggy, trackways evolved over the drier parts and forded rivers and streams at the most practical points.

TRACKWAYS

The number of trackways is large; Crossing in his *Guide to Dartmoor* lists and describes over eighty. Many of them date from ancient times, possibly from the pre-Saxon era, though not from the Bronze Age, since there seem to be none having any obvious early connection with the main sites of prehistoric habitation: if there were any systems of trackways linking these, they are now obliterated. Some of the early tracks, though usually grass-covered, are quite easily if intermittently discernible. They fall into three main categories.

Firstly there are those leading from a point often on the fringe of the moor into its depths, and then coming to an indeterminate full stop. Sometimes the nature of the surroundings may give a clue to the trackway's purpose. It may have led to reasonably succulent grazing grounds for stock, or to an area where it was customary to cut rushes or to take turves. Both Black Lane, from Bagga Tor to Walkham Head, and Blackwood Path, from Wrangaton to the upper reaches of the Erme, provided access to turf-ties and were used for bringing back the loads of peat, as the word 'black' suggests. Or the track may have led to an old quarry or mine; there are many miles of trackway on the moor serving places of former mining activity, among them

Page 161   The Powder Mills, near Postbridge: (left) One of the two stone chimney stacks; (right) One of the ruined wheelhouses, showing the middle portion which contained the wheel and through which the leat passed

Page 162 (above) *The proving mortar at the Powder Mills, used to test the strength of the gunpowder;* (below) *An archway through the embankment built in the mid-nineteenth century with the intention of connecting the trackways of the Dewerstone Quarry workings with the South Devon Railway near Goodameavy*

those to Knock Mine, beside the River Taw at the foot of Steeperton Tor, to Henroost and Hooten Wheals at Hexworthy, to Ringleshutes on Holne Moor and to nearby Huntingdon, and from Sheepstor through Eylesbarrow to Nun's Cross and Whiteworks. Many of these trackways followed the routes of more ancient ones, but their later use has often rendered them harder and more compacted; it is possible to imagine the miners footing their way along them at the beginning and end of their hard day's work. There is a very direct route from North Bovey across the saddle between Shapley Tor and Hookney Tor to Headland and Vitifer which was much used by the men who worked at those mines, and is still a right of way, as is the track over Hameldon through Grimspound.

Then there are the tracks which provided easy access between different parts of the moor, their terminal points actually upon it. One of these is the ancient Lichway, which crossed the moor from the eastern side of the Forest westwards to Lydford. Being the legislative and ecclesiastical centre of the Forest of Dartmoor, Lydford had to be visited from time to time by people who dwelt on the moor, for attendance at the courts and for receiving the sacraments of the church. This involved a journey for some of no small distance, and the Lichway was developed as providing the easiest and most direct route. Until 1260, when Bishop Bronescombe gave his permission for the inhabitants of the ancient tenements of Babeny and Pizwell, on the eastern side of the Forest, to bury their dead at Widecombe, the Lichway was customarily used for the carrying of corpses for burial at Lydford, which accounts for the derivation of the name. Though the exact route is uncertain, particularly at the eastern end, it is probable that from a crossing of the East Dart at Bellever the Lichway followed an almost due-westerly direction, fording the West Dart, Cowsic and Walkham in turn. From the fording place on the Cowsic a clearly defined track still continues past White Barrow and across Peter Tavy Great Common, and this may well be part of the original Lichway, though there may have been alternative routes for times of unfavourable weather conditions. The track's final stages to

Lydford continued by way of Willsworthy. A crossing of elongated stepping stones at a point on the River Tavy (SX 539816), laid facing up and down, rather than across, the river is believed to have been designed to assist bearers walking abreast and carrying a corpse between them.

Other early trackways beginning and ending on the moor were those habitually used for the driving of cattle. Black Lane, in the southern part of the moor, from Fox Tor southwards to the Wollake, a tributary of the Erme, enabled moormen to drive their stock between land near Fox Tor and Greenhill. This way cut through an area of extensive peat, as its name suggests, and it is possible that at times it may also have been used for peat carrying. Black Lane is marked at each end—rather surprisingly—by a railway sleeper. An ancient trackway familiar to moormen, this time in the northern area, is known as Cut Lane; it forms a pass through the blanket bog from the East Dart to the valley of the Tavy. Cut Hill is probably named from the cutting across its northern slopes which is the route's chief feature.

This area of the blanket bog has a number of other cuttings which have been helpful over the years to moormen, huntsmen and others. Some of these have developed from natural cleavages in the peat, others have been artificially made. Many of them date from the years between 1895 and 1905 and were surveyed and constructed by Frank Phillpotts, grandson of a former Bishop of Exeter, cousin of Eden Phillpotts and a keen huntsman. With local help Frank Phillpotts was responsible for easing by this means the access to Fur Tor—a favourite retreat for foxes—and with the aid of causeways providing a convenient crossing of the boggy area between Walkham Head and Tavy Head.

Causeways, though difficult to make and maintain, were a feature too of Phillpotts' Stats House—Broadamarsh cut, and also of that known as the Sandpath, across the head of Watern Combe, though this one is more ancient, having possibly been connected with earlier peat-cutting in the vicinity of Whitehorse Hill and Quintins Man. A

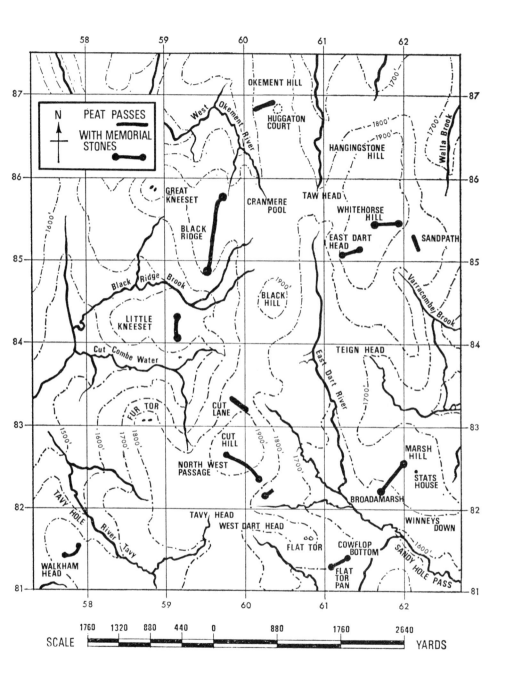

cutting known locally as the North-West Passage winds from the foot of Cut Hill almost to its summit. There are others near East Dart Head and West Dart Head, and on Black Ridge, Little Kneeset and Okement Hill, and two on Whitehorse Hill. One of these two has in recent years been widened and deepened by the action of an army bulldozer. Phillpotts took care to avoid giving the appearance of artificiality, and, following the natural erosions of the peat as the crossings invariably do, it is often hard to tell that they are man-made. However, after his death in 1909 the crossings were each marked at their ends by a bronze tablet fixed to a small granite post with the inscription:

> This stone marks a crossing through the peat, which may be of use to hunting and cattle men: the crossing was made by Frank Phillpotts, who died October 1909. It is kept up in his memory by his brother and his son.

The subject of Phillpotts peat passes has been studied by Brian Le Messurier (see Bibliography).

The third category of tracks comprises those which crossed the moor from one part of its border to another. The one probably best known to most people—by name if not by actual experience—is the Abbot's Way, so called because it provided a link between the ancient abbey at Buckfast and those at Tavistock and Buckland Monachorum. The track may, however, have originated from earlier times, even if the monks were responsible for placing a number of the crosses which mark much of its route. If so, its eastern end may well have followed a different route from the one known today, proceeding possibly from Buckfast to Horn's Cross on Holne Moor, and continuing by way of other crosses on Down Ridge, Ter Hill, Mount Misery and near Fox Tor Mire before joining the recognized route at Siward's or Nun's Cross. (The more generally considered way is from Cross Furzes, Buckfastleigh via Huntingdon Cross, Redlake and Erme Head.) From Nun's Cross the Abbot's Way proceeded westwards to Tavistock Abbey by a series of crosses as far as Whitchurch Down, while another track, branching off at Nun's Cross or before, may have continued to Buckland Monachorum by way of the Plym and Marchant's Cross. Some of this track was much used in later years by the Eylesbarrow miners. On Whitchurch Down there was probably a junction of the Tavistock branch with another route coming indirectly from Buckland through Sampford Spiney, and another, also marked by crosses, from Plympton Priory.

The name 'Abbot's Way' is in fact quite a modern one. The track was commonly known by moormen in earlier times as the 'Jobber's Path', presumably because of the yarn jobbers who travelled it with their laden pack-horses in the days of the thriving wool trade.

Crosses often served to mark the route of a trackway, but often they were used to mark a boundary. Routes might also be marked by ordinary granite guide posts. A track across the moor from Tavistock to Ashburton was marked by stones having a letter 'T' on one side and an 'A' on the other; some of the survivors can be seen on Longash Common above Merrivale, not far from the stone rows and continuing south-eastwards, and there is one just a few yards to the right of the road ascending the hill past Merrivale Bridge on the way to Princetown. These guide posts are not by any means as old as the crosses, but date probably from the late seventeenth century.

The King Way, between Tavistock and Okehampton, also dates from early times, and was in regular use until 1817, before the road which now connects the two towns was constructed. Leaving Tavistock by Old Exeter Road the early route continued west of the present road as far as Black Down, when it probably followed much the same line as that now taken, though keeping slightly to the west until after the crossing of the Lyd. Then, bearing off slightly to the east, it continued to Nodden Gate, where the Rattlebrook Peat Railway later passed beneath it, and then climbed west of Great Nodden, after which the peat railway followed the same route for a short distance. The King Way then proceeded along the dip between Corn Ridge and Sourton Tors, passing close to the site of the later ice works, and by way of Meldon eventually reached Okehampton.

In the south, too, the main route, this time from Exeter to Plymouth, passed over the fringe of the moor. Between Buckfastleigh and Harford Moor Gate it took a more northerly route than the present road.

All traffic on Dartmoor in the early days was, of course, by packhorse or donkey, much of it a concomitant of the busy tinning industry and of agricultural developments in about the thirteenth century. It is from this time that the oldest of the clapper bridges are thought to date. These structures, of large moorstone slabs supported on piers and buttresses of the same, can be found fording a number of rivers and streams, and they often indicate the crossing place of former pack-horse routes. Probably the best example of a clapper bridge is the one at Postbridge, where the old pack-horse route from Plymouth to Moretonhampstead crossed the East Dart.

ROAD-MAKING

There was very little wheeled traffic in Devon as a whole until the latter half of the eighteenth century, and certainly no roads suitable for it over Dartmoor until the making of the first turnpikes. The turnpike movement, under which local bodies comprising landowners and business men were authorised by Act of Parliament to raise capital and take responsibility for improving and maintaining lengths of road, and to collect tolls, began here around 1750. The roads around, rather than on the moor were the first to be turnpiked, with the Ashburton Trust, set up in 1755, initiating improvements towards Plymouth, and the Okehampton and Tavistock Trust following in the 1760s.

An Act for the construction of the first road over the moor, from Tavistock to Moretonhampstead via Two Bridges, was obtained in 1772, and in spite of opposition from the towns of Bodmin, Launceston and Okehampton, who felt that they would lose traffic as a result, the work was completed by the end of the century. On it were two toll gates, one at Merrivale and another at Postbridge. The making of other roads soon followed, some along routes of earlier tracks. The Ashburton to Chagford road, constructed around

1780–1800, carried a good deal of heavy traffic, mainly wagons taking wool cloth from Berry's Chagford mill to the firm's other factory at Ashburton, and bringing back lime for agricultural purposes on the return journey. A good deal of road improvement and construction went on around the borders of the moor at this time, and according to parish records many of the bridges on the lanes around the edge of Dartmoor were rebuilt (or even first built) between 1800 and 1830.

So grew up, piecemeal, the system of roads still in use today. With the heavy increase of traffic in recent years some of the original bridges built for the turnpike have proved inadequate. At Two Bridges the old one over the West Dart, built in the late 1770s or early 1780s, still stands, but a portion of the former road now simply gives access to the hotel; the newer bridge here dates from the early 1930s. And at Merrivale, too, the older bridge over the Walkham, though still remaining, has been superseded, a new one being built in 1957–8.

RAILWAYS

The first horse-drawn tramways appeared on the Dartmoor scene as early as the first quarter of the nineteenth century. The earliest, and also the first railway in Devon, was the Haytor Granite Tramway, opened in 1820. Constructed of granite rails, to connect the quarries at Haytor with the Stover Canal, this remarkable line has already been described in Chapter Four.

The Plymouth & Dartmoor Railway followed soon after, as a direct result of the development of Princetown under Sir Thomas Tyrwhitt in the preceding years. Following the peace treaty of 1815 and the subsequent departure of the French war prisoners from Princetown, trade in the area suffered a decline. Tyrwhitt, inspired with his visions of 'improving' the moor and the lives of its dwellers, conceived the idea of a railway to connect this moorland centre with the Plymouth waterside. It was to be a means of dispatching Dartmoor's exportable

commodities—granite, peat, tin and the hoped-for agricultural products—and of conveying in return lime and sea-sand for the land,
coal, timber and domestic necessities.

Plans were submitted in 1818 for the line from Princetown to
Crabtree, 2 miles from Plymouth, and in 1819 an Act incorporating
the Plymouth & Dartmoor Railway was passed. A second Act, in 1820,
authorized an extension of the line at the Plymouth end to Sutton
Pool, with a branch to Cattewater, while a third Act followed in 1821.
The line opened on 26 September 1823, though at that time its upper
end reached only as far as King Tor, in the vicinity of the granite
quarries. Due to the company's financial difficulties the final section
to Princetown was completed a little later by Messrs Johnson, who
were working the quarries under a lease (from the Lopes family)
assigned to them by the P & D Company. They acquired a mortgage
from the company to enable them to complete the job.

The railway was not the success that had been hoped. Little was
carried on it other than granite and by 1840 traffic had dwindled considerably. The Johnsons seem to have been a dominating influence
until the company settled its debts with them and regained full control in 1865. Work was done in relaying some of the track, but the
financial situation did not improve, business continued to decrease,
and eventually the section above Yelverton was sold, reconstructed
to standard gauge and reopened as the Princetown Railway in 1883.
Occasional traffic was carried on the lower part until about 1900 but
in 1916 most of the rails, with the exception of those taken over by
the Lee Moor Tramway, were removed.

The total length of the line, which was of single track throughout,
was $25\frac{1}{2}$ miles: it covered a distance as the crow flies of approximately 13 miles, which indicates the degree of winding and looping
which was necessary in this awkward terrain of hills and valleys. In
addition to the branch to Cattewater, a branch of $2\frac{1}{2}$ miles ran from
the Rising Sun, near Crabtree, to Lord Morley's Cann Quarry (part
of which, with the lower section of the line, was later to be incorporated into the Lee Moor Tramway) and another extension of the

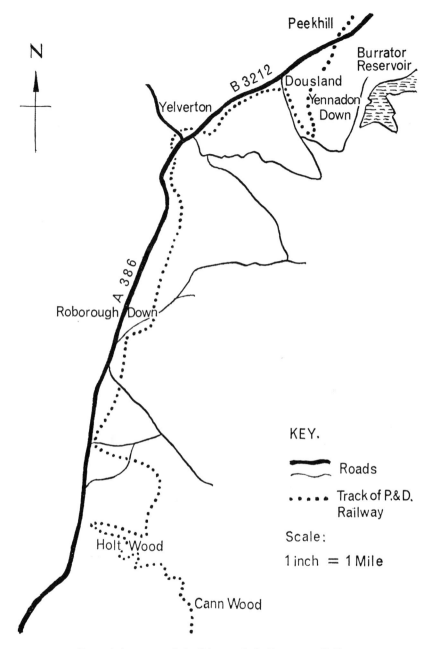

Part of the route of the Plymouth & Dartmoor Railway

Cann Quarry branch ran from Marsh Mills alongside the turnpike to Plympton.

The first part of the ascending route from Crabtree was of reasonable gradient, the construction of a tunnel at Leigham overcoming the obstacle of high ground there. This tunnel, 620 yd long, 9 ft 6 in high and 8 ft 6 in wide, was one of the earliest to be built in the country. Part of the tunnel was used as a dump after the railway was abandoned and became wet, foul and overgrown, though this did not stop its being used as an air-raid shelter in the 1939–45 war. The entrance can still be seen near Leigham (SX 515586). The tunnel is now owned by Plymouth City Council.

After the tunnel the railway took an exceedingly tortuous course through the western part of Cann Wood and through Holt Wood, contouring the land in a series of zigzags. The loops became wider, though, as the track reached Bickleigh Down, and later Roborough Down, over which it ran fairly directly due north to Yelverton. A good deal of the route across Roborough Down, where the railway and the Plymouth and Devonport leats ran almost parallel, can be clearly traced. At Yelverton the line crossed to the west of the present main road (A386) a little south of the roundabout, crossing back again immediately after it and on to the east of the Yelverton–Princetown road (B3212). The next part of its way is now covered by private gardens, until it converges, just past these, with the disused track of the later Yelverton–Princetown line. From here to Princetown the two followed much the same route (the route of the Princetown Railway is described later in this chapter), except that the Plymouth & Dartmoor kept to the west of Yennadon Down, while the Princetown Railway continued south of it and around to the east. The original terminus at Princetown was further east than the later station, and across the square, the depot later being called the Railway Arms, and more recently the Devil's Elbow.

The track of the Plymouth & Dartmoor Railway was of 4 ft 6 in gauge. The rails were of cast iron, laid in cast-iron chairs to which they were bolted, no keys being used (plate, p. 215). Throughout the main part of the line these were fixed on to granite blocks, which acted as sleepers, though the one sleeper did not support both rails. Latterly the company could not afford further chairs, so the rails were secured instead by large spikes driven into the stone. Points and crossings were also of cast iron, but the numerous sidings were of heavy granite blocks, about 4 ft in length and 1 ft wide, their inner edges specially cut to take the wheels exactly as the metal rails would do. In this respect these granite blocks differed from those on the Haytor tramway, where flangeless wheels ran on the blocks' outer edges. A number of these granite 'rails' have been incorporated into roadside curbing at Yelverton, and some of the grooved edges can be clearly seen.

Some of the later rails, which were of a different grade of metal and of cheaper construction, and the granite sleepers which supported them, are still in position and can be traced, as for example just east off the main road, ½ mile south of Yelverton (opposite the large stone mass known as 'The Rock'), where the track runs almost parallel with the road (SX 517672).

The upper section of the Plymouth & Dartmoor Railway, from Yelverton to Princetown, was bought from its owners at the time of its final decline by a private company for £22,000. Reconstructed to standard gauge it was opened as the Princetown Railway on 11 August 1883 and managed by the GWR until taken over by it in 1921.

There was no station at Yelverton until 1885; before that date connection with the Plymouth & Launceston Railway had to be made at Horrabridge. The length of the railway from Yelverton to Princetown was 10½ miles, and scenically the journey was amongst the very best that the whole of Britain could offer. As it wound its way in apparently lazy loops to climb up over the moor many points, far and near, came into view, several of them to be seen more than once, from completely different angles.

From Yelverton the railway proceeded first to Dousland, where a station was provided, then turned south to round Yennadon Down, after which a stop was made at Burrator Halt before it continued northwards again close beside and above the waters of the reservoir. Near Peak Hill the railway crossed the Yelverton–Princetown road by a bridge and started to climb over Walkhampton Common, with a stop at Ingra Tor Halt (after its opening in 1936, which benefited visitors and walkers on the moor) and then almost a complete encirclement of the area occupied by the Swell Tor and King Tor Quarries. There were sidings to serve the quarries, including the one at Foggintor, just to the north of the line, and after 1928 a halt at King Tor served a group of quarrymen's cottages there. During the circuit of King Tor the train took 15 minutes to cover a distance of 1 mile, and in ascending one could look from the window and see the other side of the loop on which one would presently travel, 200 ft above. After this the track continued eastwards to Princetown, at 1,373 ft the highest station on the GWR.

Traffic on the line in its early years was mainly concerned with the prison, which had reopened for convicts in 1850, though granite from the quarries was also carried. Latterly, however, apart from its convenience to Princetown residents, the line was largely a tourist attraction which failed to pay its way; it closed on 5 March 1956. A journey made on this line a fortnight before its closure, with the sun shining brightly out of a brilliant blue sky on a Dartmoor white with glistening snow, was one not to be forgotten. The rails were removed in 1957, and Princetown station has been largely dismantled. The area over which the track passed at Dousland has been built on, but for most of its former way the route can be easily followed.

Other tramways and railways, associated exclusively with particular industries, have been described elsewhere in the book. The system of trackways connected with the granite quarry on the Dewerstone, and the Lee Moor Tramway and Redlake Mineral Railway which both served the china-clay industry, are dealt with in Chapter Four. The tramway which brought peat into Princetown for naphtha production, and the Rattlebrook Peat Railway, as well as the Zeal Tor Tramway (constructed initially for conveying peat, though later partly used for clay), are included in Chapter Five.

Though none of the major railway developments of the nineteenth century in this region ventured into the depths of Dartmoor, some lines verged upon it and were faced with particular problems of construction due to the physical features of the moorland periphery.

Brunel's South Devon Railway, which linked Plymouth with London in 1849, touched the area in the south. From South Brent, through Wrangaton, Bittaford and Ivybridge to Cornwood, the line (later the Great Western's) closely skirted the moor's southern slopes, the lie of the land necessitating some climbing and in places the construction of viaducts. The two earlier viaducts at Cornwood and the one at Ivybridge, originally partly of timber, were replaced by the present stone ones. Some remains of the earlier construction can still be seen—at Ivybridge, just east of the station and upstream from the Stowford paper mill, the stone piers which formerly carried the broad-gauge line across the valley of the River Erme still stand, close to the present viaduct which dates from 1893; they can also be seen at Cornwood. The line was absorbed into the GW in 1876 and its gauge was changed to the standard 4 ft 8½ in in 1892.

In the 1850s the line from Plymouth to Tavistock was constructed by the South Devon & Tavistock Company, led by Lord Morley, Brunel here again being concerned in the engineering. It was completed to Tavistock in 1859 and later became the property of the South Devon Company. Branching from the main line at Marsh Mills the railway, originally broad gauge, proceeded northwards up the wooded valley of the River Plym, stopping at Plym Bridge, Bickleigh and Shaugh Bridge, and then followed the valley of the River Meavy through Clearbrook Halt to Yelverton. (Here was the junction for the Princetown Railway.) Through Horrabridge and Whitchurch the line continued to Tavistock South station and was extended to Launceston through Mary Tavy and Lydford. There were tunnels at Shaugh, Yelverton and Grenofen, and six large viaducts constructed of timber and stone piers, which were replaced between 1890 and 1910. The largest of these was the Walkham viaduct, 367 yd long and 132 ft high (plate, p. 215). Its wooden cantilevers were replaced by iron ones some time around 1890 and it was a proud local boast that the changeover was done so skilfully by the workmen that no trains had to be stopped and the normal service could run all the time. The viaduct was demolished in 1965, the line having been closed at the end of 1962.

During its life the Tavistock railway was a means of introducing many thousands of people to Dartmoor. At weekends and holiday times people would flock out from Plymouth, travelling to one or other of the small stations on its route and setting out on walks of exploration. Today, its rails removed, part of the track of the disused line is itself a fascinating walk. Stations buildings have now mostly been demolished and their sites redeveloped or, as at Yelverton, protected for nature. The once familiar arch which carried the line over the A386 road near Horrabridge station has also been removed, though the brick viaduct at Magpie remains.

The Okehampton–Lydford section of the London & South Western Railway's rival route to Plymouth around the northern and western side of Dartmoor was constructed during the 1870s. This involved a climb to 950 ft above sea level—the highest point on the system of the Southern Railway (the later owners); viaducts included the spectacular though delicately designed iron one at Meldon, high up above the West Okement river. Until 1890 the LSW trains shared the track of the GW's Plymouth–Launceston line from Lydford into Plymouth; in 1890 the narrow gauge had its own independent route from Lydford through a new Tavistock station and Bere Alston to Plymouth. The line between Okehampton and Bere Alston, rich in dramatic moorland scenery, closed to passengers in May 1968.

The Moretonhampstead & South Devon Railway, opened in 1866 from Newton Abbot to Moretonhampstead, served the eastern side of Dartmoor. After Bovey Tracey, approached along part of the route of earlier Haytor Granite Tramway, the line, climbing to its destination, followed closely the Bovey and Wray valleys, with stops at Pullabrook and Lustleigh. Besides carrying goods traffic, this too was a line used by visitors to the moor; on alighting, they continued on foot or by pony-trap, or later by buses, to places such as Haytor or Chagford. The line was bought from the South Devon Railway by the Great Western in 1878. Its busiest years were the early ones of the present century; buses and private cars slowly killed its business, and the line to Moretonhampstead closed in 1959. Now the rails have been removed and other demolition carried out. Moretonhampstead station formerly had a wooden roof, but this has now been removed and the area redeveloped for modern industrial purposes and transport storage. The centrally-situated main station building, of stone, has however been retained, and a former engine shed also still remains.

Though not in any sense moorland railways, yet coming in contact with the area tangent-wise, two other lines are worth noting. The GWR's Teign Valley railway, constructed at the end of the last century, skirted the eastern part of the area from Heathfield station on the Moretonhampstead line to connect with St Thomas, Exeter. In its early days it was used to some extent for carrying material from the local mines, but latterly business was slack and it closed in 1958. The Dart Valley line of the GWR, opened as a branch of the South Devon Railway in 1871, extended from Totnes through Buckfastleigh to Ashburton. It closed in 1958, but was subsequently bought by the Dart Valley Light Railway[1] Company, under which it has been developed as a popular tourist attraction. Though this line was a backwater for much of its later life, during its first quarter-century it carried extremely heavy freight, mainly from the woollen mills at Buckfastleigh, whose goods station received more traffic than that of many larger places such as Newton Abbot.

Ashburton station is now the only one in the area to retain the original all-over wooden roof.

OTHER FORMS OF TRANSPORT

There are no canals within the Dartmoor area, though two were concerned in carrying its products. The Stover Canal carried large quantities of granite from the quarries at Haytor, with which it was connected by the tramway, and the Tavistock Canal was constructed

[1] Now operating as the South Devon Railway.

and used mainly for the conveying of ores from the mines at Mary Tavy to the River Tamar at Morwellham.

Use was sometimes made of aerial cableways. For a short time from about 1917 onwards one was used to convey timber cut at Brimpts to Princetown. Wooden pylons set in concrete supported two wire ropes, one of which carried a cradle full of wood to Princetown, while the other returned one empty. Its construction necessitated the building of bridges over two roads, those from Princetown to Dartmeet and from Princetown to Tor Royal; the halfway mark was in a rough field close to Moorlands Farm near Tor Royal newtake. There are no obvious signs of it left today, though some of the concrete bases may remain in the ground. It was not a great success and suffered from the weather, especially from the wind in the great expanse over the Dart valley near Swincombe Meet.

At Yelverton are the singularly unattractive relics of Harrowbeer aerodrome, open during the 1939–45 war. Amongst distinguished travellers who alighted here was President Harry Truman of the United States of America when he came to Plymouth to meet King George VI in 1945.

Page 179   *Road and bridge developments (above) The thirteenth century clapper bridge over the East Dart at Postbridge with, upstream, the currently-used bridge built following the Turnpike Acts 1772; (below) The now disused turnpike bridge across the River Walkham at Merrivale, with, downstream, the modern bridge built 1957–8.*

Page 180   (above) *Recently excavated houses and barns, relics of a medieval agricultural community, on the eastern slopes of Hound Tor, Manaton;* (below) *The slopes of Challacombe, showing lynchets produced by past ploughing.*

Page 181   (above) *A circular ash house associated with farm buildings at Coombe, North Bovey;* (below) *Diagrammatic drawing of a vermin trap, with covering stone removed*

PART TWO

Gazetteer

SITES already mentioned in Part One are included here, as well as many others. It should be emphasised that inclusion of a place in this list does not necessarily imply that the public have free access, nor that an owner or occupier may be willing to give permission for viewing. Respect for all sites is requested. Some structures, including old tinners' mills, are scheduled as ancient monuments and are thus legally protected. Great care should therefore be taken to avoid disturbing or removing stones from existing remains or damaging them in any way.

The boundary of the area covered follows approximately that of the National Park, with certain additions. For instance, in the south-west a stretch of typical Dartmoor border country not within the National Park is included on account of its industrial associations. In various other localities sites just over the boundary are included if they are of relevant interest. The area is dealt with strictly in parishes, in alphabetical order (see map on p. 184). Subjects are listed within each parish where they are represented in the same order as in the foregoing chapters.

ASHBURTON
Early tinning. The town was the centre of tinning for the south-eastern area of the moor and became one of the official stannary towns in 1305.

Mining. At Ausewellwood (SX 728710), there were copper and tin workings as early as 1605. Shaft remains and deep rock cuttings can still be seen on the hillside. Whiddon (SX 757721) was worked for tin and copper in the first half of the nineteenth century. Remains consists of spoil heaps, signs of leats and a wheelpit on the hillside

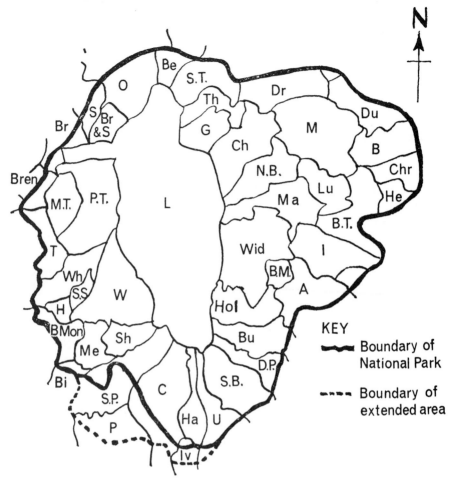

Dartmoor, showing parish boundaries

A, Ashburton; B, Bridford; Be, Belstone; Bi, Bickleigh; BM, Buckland in the Moor; B Mon, Buckland Monachorum; Br, Bridestowe; B & S, Bridestowe & Sourton Common; Bren, Brentor; BT, Bovey Tracey; Bu, Buckfastleigh; C, Cornwood; Ch, Chagford; Chr, Christow, DP, Dean Prior; Dr, Drewsteignton; Du, Dunsford; G, Gidleigh; H, Horrabridge; Ha, Harford; He, Hennock; Hol, Holne; I, Ilsington; Iv, Ivybridge; L, Lydford; Lu, Lustleigh; M, Moretonhampstead; Ma, Manaton; Me, Meavy; MT, Mary Tavy; NB, North Bovey; O, Okehampton; P, Plympton; PT, Peter Tavy; S, Sourton; SB, South Brent; Sh, Sheepstor; SP Shaugh Prior; SS, Sampford Spiney; ST, South Tawton; T, Tavistock; Th, Throwleigh; U, Ugborough; W, Walkhampton; Wh, Whitchurch; Wid, Widecombe above the Ashburn and in private grounds, where the base of an old chimney forms a circular garden pool. Druid mine (SX 745715) was probably worked for copper during the mid-nineteenth century, and had three shafts. The ruins of the stack and engine house are visible from the road to the west of Boro Wood.

For the Queen of the Dart mine (SX 734688), see p. 61; for Owlacombe and Stormsdown mines (SX 770733 etc), see p. 56.

Devon & Cornwall Umber Works. Umber, used in paint-making, was worked from the 1870s and after the turn of the century. One site was at the east end of the town, behind the hospital (SX 761705). A succession of pits were sunk and refilled after extraction of the ore, which was treated in a long shed in Balland Lane. From here the loaded carts trundled down to the station yard where there was a stamping machine. Umber was also worked at a site to the north of West Street, approximately opposite the church.

Mills. Watered by the River Ashburn (or Yeo) the town was for centuries a busy centre of the woollen industry. There were also a number of corn mills. In 1605 seven mills stood along the mill leat running through the town, though their names are not all known. Of the corn mills, Town Mills, near the town centre, now forms part of St Andrew's Close residential development for the elderly. Higher Town or Daw's Mill (west of North Street) now comprises residential flats, and the ancient Lurgecombe Mill (SX 755713), disused as such since early this century, has been converted for farming purposes.

Belford Mill (SX 754716) was an earlier woollen mill of Messrs Berry, but was converted for use as a corn mill before the middle of the nineteenth century. This ceased many years ago, and after being for long used for farming purposes the building is now converted to dwellings, and the machinery and wheelpit have disappeared. This place, sometimes locally called 'Coffin Mill' on account of its narrow shape and tapering end walls, has a striking and almost eerie appearance. Tucking or Rew Mill (SX 754706), a sixteenth-century building formerly connected with the woollen industry, is now converted for dwellings. A former woollen mill of John Berry & Sons

(p. 122) in Kingsbridge Lane has been demolished and the site is now a car park.

BELSTONE
(including STICKLEPATH)
Mining. See p. 62.
Granite working. Discarded examples of worked surface stone can be found on Belstone Common.
Mills. Cleave or Wilmotts Mill (SX 639940), powered by water conveyed by a leat from the River Taw (as were the other Sticklepath mills), dates from 1795 but is probably in fact much older. It is thought to have been originally used for corn. After a fire in 1803 it was purchased in 1810 by Messrs Pearse of Horrabridge, and rebuilt, converted and used by them for the next thirty years for the production of woollen serge. Amongst material exported from here was red cloth sent to India for the uniforms of the Nizam of Hyderabad's bodyguard. After the decline of the wool trade the mill was sold and reverted to grinding corn, continuing to operate until recent years. The main mill building has been demolished and the site re-developed.

Also at Sticklepath and strictly in SAMPFORD COURTENAY parish:
The Finch Foundry. See p. 123.
Western and Carnalls Mills, at the end of the south side of the village street, now Albany House, Mill House and Cottage, were for corn, and for bone grinding, threshing, reed combing and winnowing. Two overshot water-wheels worked in tandem. The present wheel, installed in 1972, generates electricity.
Candle factory. See p. 136.

BICKLEIGH
(Northern part only)
Mining. Bickleigh Mine (SX 517634), also called Wheal Lopes and situated in Hele Bottom Wood, produced about 20 tons of copper ore a month in the 1840s. The old shaft and workings which remain are in land let to the Forestry Commission and planted with trees.

Railway. The disused track of the GWR line from Plymouth to Tavistock, closed in 1962, can be seen along the north-eastern boundary of the parish.

BOVEY TRACEY

(the northern and western extensions of the parish only are included)

Mining. For Yarner copper mine (SX 783783), see p. 61. Of various small iron workings, most outstanding are those of Kelly Mine (SX 795818), 2½ miles north-west of Bovey Tracey on the wooded hillside. Kelly Mine Preservation Society is proceeding to restore the site which retains dressing floors and remains of buildings, with machinery including a Pelton wheel, belt transmissioning, four-head Californian stamps, winding drum with braking system and a water-wheel. Still to be seen are settling pits and narrow gauge railway track leading towards the underground workings. Working was by adits, of which seven have been located. The mine dates from the 1790s but micaceous haematite was produced mainly during the nineteenth century (notably 1879–91), and from 1900–46. More insignificant are the remains of:- Hawkmoor Mine (SX 798818), Shaptor Mine (SX 806810) and Plumley Mine (SX 804806). They are mainly overgrown and include adits and dangerous open shafts.

BRENTOR

(A broad strip along the eastern boundary of the parish is included within the area)

Railways. The adjacent routes of the South Devon & Tavistock (later Great Western) Railway from Plymouth via Lydford to Launceston (closed 1962) and the London & South Western (Southern) Railway (closed 1968) can be seen close to the River Burn, along the parish boundary, with the former Brentor Station at SX 486812.

BRIDESTOWE

(Eastern part only. Land common to the parishes of Bridestowe and

Sourton is included under SOURTON)

Mining. At Wheal Fanny or Crandford Mine (SX 521883), the walls of the engine house, of local stone with fine granite quoins, still partially stand, and around are the remains of the old workings, undulations and spoil heaps. Lead and copper were both mined here in the latter part of the nineteenth century. Originally an adit connected a line of six shafts, with two air shafts, but there has been considerable subsidence and subsequent levelling by the owner.

Railway. The Rattlebrook Peat Railway commenced its ascent at Bridestowe station, from which its route, after the crossing of the main road (on the Tavistock side of the main railway bridge SX 527876) can be traced. (Described on p. 110.)

BRIDFORD

Mining. Remains of the old Birch lead mine exist at what is now called Many Waters (SX 826871). The old stack, remains of the walls of the wheel-house and spoil dumps have been skilfully incorporated into a private garden. The mine was active in the 1850s, and is said to have been last worked about a hundred years ago. There are considerable remains of the Bridford barytes mine at SX 830865, consisting of partially demolished buildings and workings covering about 9 acres. Probably started for lead, though at a date unknown; baryte ore was mined here in 1855 until the late 1950s. Working was opencast and by shafts, the deepest of which eventually extended to about 600 ft. Old tips in the plantation on Laployd Down (SX 807850) are the remains of minor iron prospecting.

Quarrying. The Blackingstone granite quarry (SX 784858) is no longer in commercial production. Another quarry, east of the village at SX 825866, was worked by the Devon Basalt & Granite Company until 1932. Stone from it was conveyed by tramway down an inclined plane to Christow Station. Also formerly descending the hillside was an aerial ropeway which carried stone to the station from Scatter Rock Quarry on Christow Common.

BUCKFASTLEIGH

Early tinning. There are extensive remains of early tinning operations on Buckfastleigh Moor, around the source of the Wella Brook
and Mardle, and on the slopes of Snowdon. Gibby's Beam is a long
trench-like cutting and Snowdon Hole is another open working.
Some of these extended over the parish boundary to Dean Moor,
where Huntingdon Mine was worked at a later date (see under Dean
Prior).

Mining. For Brookwood Mine (SX 718675), see p. 61, and for
Kings Wood (SX 711666) see p. 69. Of the old Combe copper mine
(SX 701682), deep excavations are all that remain. In deep woodland
beside a tributary of the Dean Burn (SX 702658) are remains of
Caroline Wheal Prosper, a large wheelpit and signs of buildings, and,
about 100 yards north, an adit, with an apparent leat course from it to
the wheelpit. A depression could be the remains of Williams shaft,
originally 15 fathoms deep. Opened for tin in about 1854 it evidently
did not achieve great importance and there are no records of yields.
At SX 728658, south of Wallaford Road, is a site known locally as
'Tin Mines' but believed to have been a prospect mainly for copper
when opened as Dean Prior or Buckfastleigh Mine in 1847.
Machinery included three waterwheels (the largest of 40 ft) and
stamps, but failure in raising finance caused early cessation. The
shafts and pits are now filled.

Mills. Buckfastleigh has made full use of the River Mardle, which
flows through its midst, and the Dart, bordering the parish on the
east, to power various mills over the years. It is said that in the sixteenth century there were seven in existence in the town. For centuries Buckfastleigh has been closely associated with the wooll
industry (p. 120), and many old buildings and dwellings remain
relics of this, often glimpsed through 'opes' that give access from
streets to various courts, although it was to the town's former busy
foundry (Willcocks', north of Fore Street) that one such entrance led.
Tanning is another industry that was established close to the Mardle,
while on the Dart a paper mill (SX 747660) was operating up to the

second world war, the premises there now being occupied by other industries.

For the former Hamlyns' (later CWS) woollen mill in Chapel Street (SX 737662) see p. 122. Another woollen mill, Churchwards', stood upstream on the Mardle's north bank just above the bridge between Market Street and Bridge Street until being burnt down in 1906. Its tall chimney remained for many years before it was demolished. Some walls remain and the arched entrance from Silver Street can still be seen, also part of an old launder.

In the village of Buckfast, amongst the modern buildings and plant of Buckfast Spinning Mill (SX 742673)—the yarn spinning division of the Axminster Carpet Company—are few remaining relics of the former Buckfast Woollen Mill, which dated from when Berrys' business was moved here from Ashburton in about 1850. Most of the lower mill was destroyed by the fire of 1877, and another occurred in 1967. The natural river water is still used for both power and processing. Other buildings across the road may have been associated with the earlier woollen industry.

Higher Buckfast Mill (SX 739674), latterly works of the Buckfast Plating Company, dates from around 1800 and is believed to have been built on the side of the early woollen mill used by the Cistercian monks. A conspicuous feature at the back is the wooden launder carrying water brought from the moor by an intricate system of leats. The Holne Moor leat, from which water is still taken by various riparian owners, meeting the Holy Brook at Michelcombe, is the main source of the supply. The wheel-pit, at the south end of the building, can still be seen, but the water later worked turbines instead of the former waterwheel (see also p. 122).

The former Brook corn mill (SX 724675) is now a residence.

Railway. For Buckfastleigh Station, terminus of the Dart Valley Railway, see p. 177.

BUCKLAND MONACHORUM
(Only a crescent-shaped portion of the parish along the northern and eastern boundaries is included)

Mining. At SX 515672 etc there are few visible signs of the South Roborough Down mid-nineteenth-century copper workings, most having been virtually obliterated by the construction of Harrowbeer aerodrome. A few undulations on the west of the Horrabridge–Yelverton road, at SX 513684, mark the site of the small North Roborough Down tin mine which functioned in the early 1860s. At Poldice mine (SX 491707), the wheel-pit and the remains of some walls can be seen south of the River Walkham near Grenofen Bridge. It was worked in the 1880s, small yields of lead, copper and tin being obtained, Yeoland Consols, p. 55; Virtuous Lady, p. 60.

Water. The routes of both the Plymouth and Devonport leats can be followed for some distance over Roborough Down (see pp. 136–8).

Railway. Much of the track of the Plymouth & Dartmoor Railway is still discernible, mostly running in close proximity to the leats (see p. 169), also some of the route of the former South Devon & Tavistock (later Great Western) Railway which passed by tunnel beneath Yelverton village.

CHAGFORD
Early tinning. Chagford was a stannary town, appointed in 1305 as one of the official places for the weighing and stamping of tin.

There are remains of tinners' workings along the South Teign with ruins of a blowing-house at Outer Down (in private grounds) and another tin mill opposite Thornworthy.

Mining. At SX 713875, remains of the open workings and shafts mark the site of the Greatweek mine, which was restarted for tin in the 1880s on the site of earlier workings. On the western side of the Birch Tor-Vitifer area are:- West Vitifer (SX 679828) with dumps and remains of wheelpits and buddles from tin workings of the 1850s to '70s; Bushdown (SX 680818) whose openwork runs close to the B 3212 road; and King's Oven and Waterhill (SX 675812) where a series of cuttings remain from nineteenth century and older workings. (King's Oven is not now regarded as an ancient smelting place.)

Mills. The beautiful old Holy Street Mill (SX 688878), with walls of stone and a thatched roof, dates from the late eleventh century and was formerly a corn mill. The waterwheel has been restored and used in the production of electricity for the nearby house and outbuildings. Water from the River Teign supplies the leat. At Yeo Mill (SX 679866) electricity is also generated by means of a wheel, worked by water from the South Teign. This was of life-long pride to Mr Wallace Perryman, who, in his nineties, died in recent years. The mill was probably built at about the time that his ancestors came to live and farm at Yeo in 1545. In its early days it was used for grinding corn, and for threshing, but was later adapted for a variety of purposes. The present overshot waterwheel replaced an earlier all-wood one which was removed in 1877. The wheel in use now is of 13 ft diameter, 40 in wide, and has wrought-iron buckets, a wooden belly and arms, metal rims and a metal shaft, and has a capacity of 600 cu ft a minute.

Besides crushing oats and working mechanical devices for the farm and smithy, the wheel's power has driven a circular saw, a lathe and other equipment associated with sawmilling. Also, the wheel has been used for over ninety years for generating electricity. The original plant producing 100 volts was installed, and the house, farm buildings and mill lit, Mr Perryman remembered, on the evening of 4 January 1893. As such it was one of the earliest electrical power plants on record. Subsequently larger generators were installed to deal with ever increasing loads. The present wheel is geared to take a dynamo supplying the farm and outbuildings with direct lighting of 110 volts.

Sandy Park Mill (SX 713893) ceased to be a corn mill in about 1917 and is now the Mill End Hotel. The leat and waterwheel, used for producing hydro-electricity in the 1930s, are well preserved. Posts in the dining-room are part of the original mill, and there are some mill-stones in the garden.

The old buildings of Rushford Mill (SX 706884) are now used for agricultural purposes, though corn was ground until 1947. The wheel is no longer in position, its wooden parts having been used to strengthen the river banks. Stepping-stones across the river were formerly used by men carrying sacks of corn to the mill from a nearby threshing place. The leat still carries water. Batworthy Mill (SX 714852), a former corn mill by the River Bovey, has been disused for about fifty years. The old buildings and parts of the former wheel and machinery remain, but some restoration has been carried out, including a new waterwheel for possible use in generating electricity. Water still runs in the leat.

For woollen mills, see p. 119.

CHRISTOW

Mining. Considerable remains exist both above and below ground in the Teign valley from mid-nineteenth century mining for lead, silver, zinc and blende. The mines comprised: Wheal Exmouth (SX 837830) at Canonteign, with Wheal Adams (Reed Mine) to the north. Over 12,000 tons of 65 per cent lead ore were produced here from 1845–74, together with silver, zinc and some copper, and in 1870 twenty people were employed. The most prominent remains are large spoil heaps on both sides of the B 3193 road, while behind them, beside the minor road near Canonteign Barton, stands the noble ivyclad ruin of an engine house and chimney, constructed in ornamental style for aesthetic reasons to preserve the view from Canonteign House. Finely cut granite features in its masonry, which includes impressive archwork. Frankmills (SX 835821), at Hyner, was larger, producing nearly 15,000 tons of 67 per cent lead ore, and silver, barytes, fluorspar, haematite and spathic ore from 1856–80. Very large tips remain at this site, and some ruins include an engine house and chimney. Water from the impressive waterfalls, which are partly natural and partly manmade, was used for washing ore from the mines.

Shuttamoor Mine (SX 823829) was a small working for iron (micaceous haematite), operated between the 1880s or '90s and 1911. There is little to be seen but shafts and the remains of adits.

Quarrying. Basalt was worked at Scatter Rock Quarry (SX 822855) on Christow Common until 1950. The stone was conveyed down an incline to an aerial ropeway which carried it to the former Christow Station (SX 840865).

CORNWOOD

Early tinning. There are remains of tinners' workings along the Erme, the right bank of which is in this parish, and also along the Yealm. Of particular note on the Erme are the excavations known as Erme pits, SX 624668. Some way downstream are the remains of a tinners' hut. There are two ruined blowing-houses on the Yealm, one on each side of the river, one being above and the other below the fall in its course known as Yealm Steps.

China-clay working. For the Cholwich Town and Heddon Down areas see pp. 86–94.

Mills and Farming. Fardel Mill (SX 604573), formerly a corn mill, now comprises a farm and dwellings, and signs of milling have disappeared. Wisdome Mill (SX 614608) was also a corn mill but is now a private house. There are still remains of the waterwheel, but the leat is dry. Wisdome Farm (SX 615603) is one of several ancient farmhouses in the parish. The present dwelling is believed to date from the sixteenth century, but beside it are parts of an even older building, with fine granite mullions and door posts. In one of the fields of Wisdome Farm is 'New Barn' (SX 621599), an old (re-roofed) stone building with granite quoins and lintels. Still in position outside is an iron waterwheel (approx 14 ft), and some machinery still survives from when winnowing, reed combing, threshing and grinding were done here. Water was held in a pond and piped to the launder for the wheel. Beside the building, set in rows, are fifteen granite stack stools (without 'mushroom' tops). Blachford Mill (SX 616600), formerly a sawmill, retains some ironwork of the old waterwheel, machinery and launder.

DEAN PRIOR

Early tinning. Remains of early tinners' workings can be found, particularly in the vicinity of the Brockhill Water, a tributary of the Avon which now discharges into the Avon reservoir.

Mining. Huntingdon Mine (SX 670670) is a remnant of workings which extended into the northern end of the parish from Buckfastleigh Moor. The mine was being worked early in the nineteenth century when it was known as Devon Wheal Vor, but was probably abandoned by 1815. It reopened in about 1862, small quantities of tin being obtained. The overgrown remains of two wheel-pits, parts of the courses of the leats which supplied them from the West Wella Brook, and sites of buildings can be traced. No adits or shafts are visible but a line of funnel-shaped pits may have been sunk for the purpose of exploring the lode, and possibly served to ventilate the mine.

Mill. Dean Mill (SX 733648) was a corn mill up to the 1930s. It is now solely a dwelling and Dean Burn water no longer flows in the leat.

DREWSTEIGNTON

Mining. Bradford Pool (SX 700910) marks the site of tinning excavations from the sixteenth century. Water for power and ore processing was brought along a 12-mile leat from Watern Combe, across Gidleigh and Throwleigh Commons, which became a matter of dispute and of litigation in the seventeenth century. It is believed that the present pool owes its existence to adits becoming blocked during the nineteenth century.

Mills. Vete Mill (SX 735916) was for wood-working, the leat still carries water. Furlong Mill (SX 709895) is now a residence.

DUNSFORD

Mills. For Steps Bridge Edge Tool Mills (SX 807884), see p. 124. The former Dunsford flour mill (SX 811887) is now a private house. The waterwheel was removed in the 1940s.

GIDLEIGH

Early tinning. There is considerable evidence of tinners' workings along the North Teign, Walla Brook and Rue Lake.

Mill. Old Gidleigh Mill (SX 674887) is now a farm.

HARFORD

Early tinning. Evidence of tinners' workings lies along the valley of the Erme, the left bank of which is in Harford parish. Remains of a tinners' mill can be seen close to the junction of Dry Lake and the Erme (SX 640634), and of another near the point where Hook Lake flowing from Stony Bottom (also the scene of past tinning activity) enters the river, SX 639651. There is also a ruined tinners' mill on the left bank of the Butterbrook.

China-clay working. There are remains of clay working at Left Lake (SX 647634 etc) and the parish boundary in the north borders on the Redlake clay area (see p. 95).

Railway. The disused Redlake Mineral Railway track meanders in and out of the parish (see p. 96).

HENNOCK

Mining. South Exmouth Mine (SX 836808), marked by vegetated dumps on both sides of the road above Teign Village, produced lead and silver from 1862–7. Very small quantities of these metals were produced at Hennock Mine (SX 837816) from 1836–55 where dumps remain. For Great Rock Mine (SX 827815) see p. 68. Bowden Hill Mine (SX 819809) (micaceous haematite) is marked by surface workings.

HEXWORTHY—see LYDFORD

HOLNE

Mining. At SX 674698, on Holne Moor, in the vicinity of Holne Ridge, a number of old cuttings and deep gullies, and signs of an engine house, wheelpit and leats remain from tin-working at

Page 197 (above) *Nun's Cross Farm in 1967. The smaller building on the right, which no longer stands, built in 1870 and originally thatched, was the farmhouse until superseded some years later by the other;* (below) *The walls and undulations marking the site of Sourton iceworks*

Page 198 (above) *Water in the Devonport leat still flows as far as the Meavy valley, tumbling down Raddick Hill and crossing the River Meavy by an iron launder;* (below) *The Reddaford leat, carrying water from the River Tavy, formerly served the mines at Mary Tavy; now it supplies the power station there. At the point shown here, near Nat Tor, as the water flows toward one it gives the uncanny impression of running uphill*

Ringleshutes, worked latterly from 1852. It is said that a chimney remained here in 1880, but by 1900 the site was long deserted. Of Holne Chase Mine (SX 724716) there is little to see; it produced small quantities of tin in the 1870s. The site on the hill is overgrown, but three adits are visible from the river. In Combestone Wood, SX 672723, are remains comprising openwork, pits, walls and dressing floors, of Wheal Cumston, a nineteenth century tin mine sited on earlier workings.

The now dry channel of the Wheal Emma leat (see p. 61) can be seen on Holne Moor. It entered the parish where its course crossed the O Brook and meandered north and south again to encircle Combestone Tor and Holne Moor, crossing the Hexworthy–Holne road four times in the process, and continuing west of the village of Holne to the valley of the Mardle.

Mill. Ruined ivyclad walls are all that now remain of Holne corn mill (SX 714685) by the Holy Brook.

Holne Moor leat—see p. 190.

HORRABRIDGE

Early tinning. Many mortar stones and other granite relics, discovered during rebuilding, are preserved in the garden of 'Tinners' Mill', Little Horrabridge (SX 514695).

Mining. For Wheal Franco see p. 60. Sortridge Consols Mine (SX 510707), formerly West Wheal Robert, is marked by large dumps east of the old Horrabridge–Tavistock road. It was reopened in 1853 and worked profitably for copper until 1868, and some tin was produced 1883–1902. The adjacent North Wheal Robert (SX 513708), which incorporated East Wheal Robert (SX 518706), produced mainly copper ore from 1853–68. Water from the Grimstone and Sortridge leat was used. Dumps now remain. Dumps and dangerous shafts in woods on the border with Walkhampton (SX 515692) are remains of Furzehill Mine, worked during the 1860s and '70s for tin and arsenic. Eight men were drowned in a flood in 1866 when drilling from one of the levels pierced old water-filled workings, (see p. 57).

Mills. Mill remnants exist in residential properties west of Foxhams (SX 516698) where, on the site of earlier corn, fulling and serge mills, premises were rebuilt around 1840 as a serge factory by Gill, Rundle and Bridgman of Tavistock, taken over by Hamlyn and Co. of Buckfastleigh in 1873. Demolition followed the 1890s decline in wool, and the premises were used for some time as a sawmill. At Phoenix (SX 514694) mills for various purposes have existed over centuries—corn, fulling, leather, paper from 1788, wool in 1810, and from 1819 corn again. The mill was burnt down in 1969 and the premises are now a joinery works. The Mill, beside the river at the bridge in the village (SX 513699) housed a wheelwright's business and, from 1914–47, an electrical generating station.

Brickworks. This occupied a site near Bedford Bridge at Magpie, SX 513703, where there were also claypits during the nineteenth century.

ILSINGTON

Mining. On either side of the Haytor–Widecombe road, just east of Hemsworthy Gate (SX 744761), the surface remains of Hemsworthy Mine can be seen, forming a typical open-cast cut. Mining was carried on here intermittently during the mid-nineteenth century on the site of the former workings of the 'old men'; production of 16 tons of black tin was recorded for 1853–5. Working was by shallow underground levels; adits and shafts are now filled. On the site of Bagtor Mine (SX 765759) are remains of buildings, dressing floors and a large wheelpit. A 60 ft waterwheel was here in 1862. Above, on the down, are old surface workings and remnants of shafts and adits. Small quantities of tin were produced, probably early in the 1860s.

At SX 772770 & 772773, south of Haytor Vale, can be seen a deep cutting and an adit which formed part of the Haytor Iron Mine. There is also an adit east of the Vale amid beech trees, at SX 773773 (see p. 68). Atlas and Smallacombe mines may at times have been connected with the Haytor Iron Mine, being on the same magnetic beds.

Smallacombe opencast cutting, SX 777766, is very overgrown. Various shafts, including some in the grounds of a private house near Lewthorne Cross, SX 779762, were part of Atlas Mine, worked in the mid-nineteenth century for iron and in later years for tin. One of these, White's Shaft, incorporated into a garden and grown over with shrubs, fenced around, is open and said to be square and 35 fathoms deep; it was used by the Albion Company, who worked the mine for about five years in the 1920s, when tin, copper and arsenic were produced. Nearby, in a copse, are the concrete beds of the engine which worked the compressor at that time, the plant and building having been removed. There are also various dumps, some covered with trees. It is said that there were stamps at Trumpetor around 1900.

Nothing remains to be seen of Sigford Consols copper and tin mine which was situated about a mile north of Sigford hamlet, on the east side of the River Lemon, SX 774751. After its working ceased, probably in the late 1860s, stone from the engine house was used for building Lewthorne cottages. Nor are there signs of Smith's Wood tin and copper mine (SX 773748), but in Smith's Wood are the remains of burning-houses with flues up through the wood to an ivy-covered tower-like stack, about 6 ft in diameter. Remains of other features exist in the landscaped garden of the restored cottages.

For Silverbrook Mine (SX 789759), see p. 66.

Manganese was also obtained in the Ilsington area in the early part of the nineteenth century.

Granite working. For the Haytor granite quarries and tramway, see p. 77.

Mill. Bagtor Mill (SX 769755), an old corn mill, with more modern wheel, is now a private house.

IVYBRIDGE

Mills. For the Stowford paper mill, see p. 128.

Railway. For Brunel's viaduct on the former South Devon Railway, see p. 175.

LUSTLEIGH

Mining. Peck Pits (SX 763833) signs of ground disturbance are evidence of past tinworking, but no details are known.

Mill. Lustleigh Mill (SX 786809), a former corn mill, has been converted to a dwelling house. The wheel has gone, but water still rushes down at the side of the building.

Railway. The disused track of the Moretonhampstead Railway passes near the village and continues north and north-west.

LYDFORD

Owing to its large size this parish is dealt with under four headings: LYDFORD (NW), PRINCETOWN, POSTBRIDGE and HEXWORTHY.

LYDFORD (North-west)

(The area north of the Tavy and Teign)

Early tinning. The square keep of Lydford Castle (SX 509847), much of which still remains standing imposingly on a hillock on the edge of the village, was built in 1195 as a prison for offenders against Forest and Stannary laws. It was notorious for the harsh treatment meted out within its walls, often before or without proper trial.

There is evidence of early tinners' workings along the banks of the River Lyd on the moor, and also beside the River Taw.

There are the remains of a tinners' mill with fine mouldstone at SX 637842, on the left bank of the North Teign near the old abandoned Teignhead Farm.

Mining. At the foot of the western slopes of Steeperton Tor, beside the infant River Taw (SX 615884), are the remains of Steeperton Tor or 'Knack' Mine, which was active for tin during the nineteenth century on the site of earlier workings, up to the 1880s. The remains, recently investigated by Dr T. A. P. Greeves, include a hillside reservoir, gullies, adits, shafts and pits, parts of a dam across the Taw, a leat, wheelpit and buddle site, as well as building ruins. Of Wheal Mary Emma (SX 532852), some prominent undulations and

remains of stonework can be seen along the banks of the Lyd, about
1½ miles east of Lydford village, in the valley between High Down
and Brat Tor. Tin was formerly worked here on a small scale. In the
valley of the Doetor Brook (a tributary of the Lyd) between Brat Tor
and Rattlebrook Hill, is the site of the small Foxhole tin mine or
Wheal Frederick (SX 546854, plate p. 23). Close to a ruined two-
roomed building set in this extensive operwork are the remains of two
wheelpits, a launder base, and two circular buddles. Further downstream are remains of shafts, adits and leats. Remains are also
apparent of Rattlebrook Mine, or Wheal George, (SX 560857),
another small tin mine east of the Rattlebrook, between Rattlebrook
Hill and Amicombe Hill. Wheal Prosper (SX 573793) in the
Walkham's upper reaches, is marked by openworks, remains of
buildings and signs of other features; tin was worked here in the
nineteenth century.

Peat cutting. Remains of the peat-charcoal industry, 'meilers' and
crude granite kilns can be seen in the north of the area, particularly
near Wild Tor, as well as various tracts of peat-denudation (see p.
100). The remains of many shelters for peat-cutters, or others, are to
be found in remote situations of the high moor (see p. 101).

For Rattlebrook Peatworks (SX 560871), see p. 109.

LYDFORD (PRINCETOWN)
(The area south of the Tavy, west of the Dart and Swincombe)

Mining. For Whiteworks (SX 612710), see p. 46. In addition to
the mine here, the area was a centre of habitation for miners and
agricultural workers. Bachelors Hall Mine was at SX 599736, but
few signs remain; small quantities of tin were worked in the early
part of the nineteenth century. Of Nun's Cross tin mine (SX 602699
etc) there are various remains, in the form of cuttings and undulations, both east of Nun's Cross Farm around the headwaters of the
Swincombe and extending into Walkhampton parish to the north and
west as far as Crazy Well Pool. Also there are workings further south,
close to the upper reaches of the Plym, SX 607684. Yields were evi-

dently small, and there are no records of production.

Peat cutting. The scars of peat cutting are to be found at various places, including the site of the former Walkham Head Peatworks (see p. 105). About 250 yd east of Rendlestone Cross (SX 578750) are signs of a now-grassy track, north and south of the road, which curves away around the plantation on the prison ground in the direction of Princetown. This formed a section of the route of a tramway over which peat was brought in to supply the Princetown naphtha works (see p. 106).

Farm. Nun's Cross Farm (SX 606698) was the last smallholding to be taken in from the moor and was of about thirty acres. John Hooper was the pioneer here and he built the original dwelling house for his wife and two children in about 1870 with his own hands, living meanwhile in a makeshift shelter of rocks and rushes. He converted the surrounding area from heather to a grassy sward which he cut for hay. The remains of Hooper's house have now mostly been removed, with only the outer and inner wall footings still marking the site. Beside it stands the three-bedroomed house which superseded it, built at the end of the century by his son-in-law and daughter, a Mr and Mrs Worth, who raised thirteen children there.

Stone walls. Many of the stone walls in the vicinity of Two Bridges are relics of the enclosing of land in the late eighteenth century and early part of the nineteenth (see p. 153).

Bridge At Merrivale (SX 550751), see pp. 84 and 169 (plate, p. 179).

Railway. Princetown was the terminal point of the Plymouth & Dartmoor Railway and of the later Princetown line. The depot for the former was on the site of the Devil's Elbow Hotel, while the later railway station, now completely dismantled, was just to the west of the village (see pp. 169–74).

LYDFORD (POSTBRIDGE)

(South of the North Teign, east and north of the West Dart)

Early tinning. At Crockern Tor (SX 616758), from 1305 onwards, were held the Stannary Parliaments for Devon, at which all matters relating to stannary laws were discussed and grievances raised. The last occasion was probably in the year 1749. After that date the tor was used as a quarry, when stone removed probably included slabs of granite formerly used by the parliament as 'tables' and 'chairs'.

There is evidence of tinners' workings at numerous places on the banks of the rivers, including mill remains at two places near tributaries of the East Dart—one near the Stannon Brook between Ringhill and Hartland Moor, the other on the right bank of the Wallabrook, near Runnage.

Mining. At Brimpts (SX 668738) a small tin mine operated in the 1850s, but little can be seen of it now. A small area of workings on the western edge of the large Birch Tor–Vitifer mining area lies within Lydford parish. These include cuttings and dumps beside the B3212 road opposite the Warren House Inn, and on the other side of the road, west of the inn, the remains of a small mine, Wheal Caroline (SX 668808), with the ruins of a miner's house.

The Vitifer mine leat, about 7 miles in length, was constructed in about 1830 to bring in water from the East Dart. Either at the same time or rather later the flow was supplemented by water led in from the North Teign. Like some of the other leats it is crossed at a number of places by simple stone clapper footbridges. The point of intake of the East Dart is at SX 625812, on the north bank of the river near Sandy Hole. Contouring the hillsides the leat takes a tortuous north-easterly course, continuing south of Sittaford Tor before being joined by its tributary from the North Teign. Presently it swings to the south and passes under the Two Bridges–Moretonhampstead road (B3212) less than a mile south-west of the Warren House Inn. It then flows into the Vitifer area, after which the water eventually finds its way to the West Webburn and back to the Dart at a lower point.

Mills. For the Powder Mills (SX 628769 etc), see pp. 128–33.

Warrening. There are remains of a rabbit warren, dating probably from the last part of the nineteenth century, on the hillside on the east side of the West Dart, in the area between Wistman's Wood and Longford Tor. The eleven buries in a line above the wood and another west of the tor differ from others on the moor in having no ditches around their upper ends. Also visible are the remains of the warrener's hut: on a level platform dug into the hillside rests a rectangular layer of stone outlining its extent. The remainder of the building, now removed, was of wood.

Bridges. For the clapper bridge at Postbridge (SX 648789), see p. 168 (plate, p. 179). There are the remains of another bridge of the same type at Bellever (SX 658773). The old bridge at Two Bridges (SX 608749) is mentioned on p. 169.

LYDFORD (HEXWORTHY)
(Area east of the Swincombe, south of the Dart)

Early tinning. Evidence of tinning activity is found along the banks of the Swincombe and Dart, and also around the upper reaches of the Avon and Erme, which lie within the area. Two tinners' mills at Week Ford, on the West Dart, are described on p. 32. There are remains of others at Gobbet on the Swincombe, and on the left bank of the Avon, below Henglake, while the possible remains of two others are to be found on the Blacklane Brook or Wollake, a tributary of the upper Erme. Fox Tor Gert, a deep and extensive cutting on the eastern and southern slopes of Fox Tor, is a good example of an open gully made and left by the tinners.

Mining. For the Hexworthy mines (Henroost and Hooten Wheals), see p. 50. Open cuttings and dumps are all that remain of the Gobbet tin mine (SX 647728), which operated in the mid-nineteenth century. Much of the stone from its buildings was used in the construction of the Swincombe reservoir. After earlier working and a probable spell of inactivity, machinery was installed in 1865, following which working continued until the 1870s. Yields were small.

The dry channel of the Wheal Emma leat (see p. 61), which took in water from the Swincombe at a weir just east of Whiteworks, at SX 623710, contours the hillside eastwards above the valley.

China-clay working. For the Redlake clayworks and mineral railway, see pp. 95–7.

Peat cutting. Time has obliterated most of the signs of the extensive peat cutting carried on at Redlake in the 1840s from which the naphtha works at Shipley Bridge was supplied (see p. 109).

Farm. Fox Tor Farm, SX 629706—see p. 154.

Warrening. Huntingdon Warren, of about 610 acres in the area of the Avon and Western Wella Brook, was enlarged and developed in the early part of the nineteenth century apparently on the site of an earlier warren. Four small vermin traps have been found here, all within and against a possible boundary wall. Many buries can be seen, but the warren house, on the eastern side, was destroyed some years ago.

MANATON

Early tinning. For the tin-streaming pond at SX 691802, see p. 25.

Mining. The Golden Dagger Mine (SX 682803), situated east of the Walla Brook, in the northern part of Soussons Down, is the only one of those forming part of the important Birch Tor–Vitifer area (see p. 46) to lie within Manaton parish. It was worked from 1879 onwards by Mr Moses Bawden, and at times 30–40 men were employed. From intermittent working between 1882 and 1914 the production of 220 tons of black tin was recorded. An adit was cut into the hillside, and three shafts connected the underground levels with the surface. The remains are now covered by a forestry plantation. For Buddles (SX 686796), see p. 45.

Mills. East corn mill (SX 750808) has long been disused as such. Water Mill (SX 758807) is undergoing restoration as a dwelling, and the leat, launder and wheelpit remain. It is believed to have served mainly farming needs (threshing etc), and possibly sawmilling.

Farming village. Hound Tor 'village' is at SX 746790; see p. 146.

Challacombe field systems. Early field systems marked by lynchets, on the eastern side of Challacombe Down, are particularly conspicuous in the light of early evening when the sun shines down on the hill-slope (see p. 147).

MARY TAVY

Mining. Wheal Friendship (SX 508794) is discussed on p. 58. The central area of former operations today presents a generally derelict scene, although some of the waste material has been removed in recent years and the former mine captain's house and count house have been restored for habitation, as also have nearby miners' cottages. On the opposite side of the road are the ruins of the arsenic works—various buildings and the remains of the condensing chambers (see plate p. 54, pp. 58–9 and pp. 64–5).

The site of the small South Friendship copper mine (SX 509783) is now occupied by the hydro-electric station of National Power. Working was in the early part of the nineteenth century, though in later years quantities of arsenic were recovered from the waste material. At North Betsy (SX 512823), the remains of an old shaft and working close beside the main road, to the west, are the probable relics; zinc was produced in the 1850s. At SX 503809, old shafts and surface workings on Gibbet Hill, west of the main road across Black Down, are the remains of unsuccessful trials for tin dating from about 1870. Remains of Wheal Jewell's workings and shafts can be found on Horndon and Kingsett Downs, and near them is now situated the reservoir for the Mary Tavy power station (see p. 141). Wheal Jewell (SX 525813) was opened for tin in 1865 on the site of earlier workings and was in production as recently as 1911 and 1924, in the later years being worked in conjunction with Wheal Friendship. Arsenic was also produced. Wheal Betsy (SX 510812) is discussed on p. 65.

Mill. Wortha Mill (SX 485803), a former grist and flour mill by the River Burn, has been disused as such since the 1920s or '30s. The existing building, probably over 200 years old, is believed to occupy the site of an earlier mill. It now serves farming needs. The wheelpit and leat remain.

MEAVY

Early tinning. There is considerable evidence of tinners' workings in the southern part of the parish, particularly near the Plym, east of Cadover Bridge in the vicinity of Brisworthy. It is believed to have been in this area in the twelfth century that the Dartmoor tinning industry had its beginnings (frontispiece). There are blowing mill remains just upstream from Cadover Bridge, on Brisworthy Burrows (SK 560646). Greenwell Gert is a pronounced openwork on the north-west edge of Wigford Down.

Mining. At SX 534637, in Dewerstone woods, just east of the River Meavy and almost opposite Grenoven, are mounds and tumbled walling of a ferro-ceramic mine. The ore was used in brick-making but was probably of poor quality. In the grounds of Yennadon House and on Yennadon down are overgrown dumps and cuttings which are the remains of opencast workings for iron ore (SX 544682 etc).

Granite working. For the Dewerstone Quarry (SX 536642), and also trackways and embankment (SX 531645) connected with it, see p. 85.

China-clay working. Pits and mounds from past clay working can be seen on the east side of Wigford Down.

Mill. Meavy corn mill (SX 539672), situated in the village, ceased to work at about the time of the Great War. After lying derelict it was converted to a dwelling-house several years ago. The wheel has long since disintegrated, the only relic of the original mill being the flight of stone steps leading up to the front door.

Railways. Remains of both the Plymouth & Dartmoor Railway and the Princetown Railway are on Yennadon Down. The former line ran northwards on the west side of the down, while the latter circled it in an anti-clockwise direction (see pp. 169–74).

MORETONHAMPSTEAD

Mining. Iron ore (micaceous haematite) was worked in the 1930s by adits at Moorwood Mine (SX 777838), where dressing sheds are now a private house, and in the 1920s and '30s at Wray Mine (SX 771848). At Wray, near a public footpath, can be seen dressing floors, three buddles, wall remains and tramway tracks to adits.

Mills. Steward Mill (SX 764852), preserved to display various features including a new waterwheel; Doccombe Mill (SX 781871) and one at Clifford Bridge (SX 780897)—both now without signs of milling but called 'Mill House'; and Fingle Mill (SX 745897) whose ruins containing metal parts bearing the name 'Dicker, Chagford' lie downstream from Fingle Bridge (it was burnt down in 1894) were all for corn. Wool was important in the town for centuries, with a fulling mill by 1300 (sited at the bottom of Lime Street, left by the stream SX 755862) and some town buildings were associated with the later cloth trade.

Railway. For the Moretonhampstead Railway see p. 176.

Tollhouse. A good example near the former station (SX 759857).

NORTH BOVEY

Early tinning. Evidence of early tinners' workings in the western extremity of the parish include gullies near Headland. Above, on the slopes of Hookney Tor (SX 699811), can be seen something of the system of leats used for conveying water from Grim's Lake for the streaming operations (see p. 25).

Mining. The greater part of the Vitifer–Birch Tor area lies within this parish (see p. 46). To the east of this was the smaller Headland Mine (SX 694811), active in the 1860s on the site of earlier workings. Very conspicuous over the hillside are the long deep scars left by the mining operations. East Vitifer tin mine (SX 708823) was worked from the 1860s to '80s. Ascending from West Combe to Combe Down remains of dressing floors and a wheelpit are seen in a wood on the left, with portals from a wheelpit drain and an adit. On the down are dangerous shaft remains and the route of a tramway from the drawing adit.

Of Great Wheal Eleanor (SX 735833), some undulations and the remains of a wheel-pit in very boggy ground on Easdon, south-west of North Bovey village, are all that remain. Tin was produced, mainly during the 1870s. Grass-covered mounds and gullies and a few lumps of tin ore lying around mark the site of the Barracott surface workings for tin (SX 740819).

Mills. New Corn Mill (SX 737837) the manor mill, disused pre-1914 and now a store attached to a dwelling house, still retains its waterwheel—supporting climbing roses. Its former leat is now a footpath. Bowden Corn Mill (SX 724841), worked up to the 1940s, stands in a range of buildings with the wheel still in position, and with water in the leat. Buildings at Blackaller Farm (SX 738838) were once a woollen mill.

Ash houses. Opposite the former woollen mill just described is a circular ash house. There is another, in very good repair, at Thorne (SX 725854), and others, also circular, at West Combe (SX 709825) and Shapley (SX 714830).

Warrening. Headland Warren covered about 590 acres east of the Walla Brook on the southern slopes of Birch Tor. The small warren house still stands. Several vermin traps have been located.

OKEHAMPTON

Mining. Remains of Forest, Homerton and Meldon Mines (SX 561912) are now covered by the area of the Meldon reservoir. In Halstock woods, on the west side of the East Okement (SX 607936) are remains of minor workings, probably for copper or lead. There were also attempts at copper and lead working in Courtenay's Okehampton Park from the early eighteenth century, but few signs remain.

Peat cutting. The remains of the charcoal-peat industry can be seen around High Willhays (see p. 100).

Mills. A mill paying 6s 8d a year is mentioned in Domesday. Probably this was one of two mills on the East Okement, both of which were manorial, one being the double mill known as Town Mills (SX 590949), and the other in North Street. Work ceased at Town Mills in about 1955; the large mill building is now being converted to flats. The wheel and launder are still in position beside it and the water is used for generating electricity. Buildings opposite, and an old chimney, served as a bone mill and chemical fertiliser works until being used for warehousing and storage. The North Street Mill has been demolished but its leat and wheelpit are traceable. Between these two sets of mills was another whose final use was to house the town's first generating station; its weir is still across the river.

On the West Okement the weir of Clapps Mill can still be seen below the bridge with the leat traceable on the right side; the mill has disappeared, but the tunnel for the tail race can be seen from the bridge at the bottom of Market Street; there were both corn and woollen mills here in the seventeenth century.

The Museum, in Fore Street, which contains artefacts of local industries, was itself a corn mill, called Newcombe's, built in 1811. Latterly it was occupied by agricultural merchants. A bag hoist is preserved.

A large brick building in Market Street was a boot factory from the 1880s to early 1900s.

Glassworks. The site of the glassworks, and the granulite quarry which supplied the raw material and is still used, can be seen in the Meldon valley (see p. 135).

Tramway. The track of a tramway which ran from a small quarry at Fatherford to the vicinity of Okehampton railway station, passing under Fatherford Viaduct, is now a public footpath. The tramway was in use in the 1890s when the stone was used for building purposes in the town.

Railway. For Meldon viaduct (SX 564923) see p. 176.

PETER TAVY

Early tinning. There are the ruins of a tinners' mill with a good mouldstone on the right bank of the Walkham above Merrivale (SX 551766), see p. 32.

Mining. At Hillbridge Consols (SX 534806) there is little to see of mining operations, though three shafts were sunk, apparently as an unsuccessful trial for tin. Kitts or Skitts Mine (SX 516846), in the Lyd valley just east of Lydford village, was worked for lead by three shafts in the mid-nineteenth century. The shafts are filled but mounds are prominent. Other mining remains lie along the left bank of the Tavy below Horndon Bridge and above Devon United, where there were some unimportant copper prospects. For Devon United Mines, see p. 56.

The Reddaford leat, bringing water from the River Tavy, was constructed probably early in the nineteenth century to supplement the Cholwell Brook for serving the big mines at Mary Tavy—Wheal Jewell, Wheal Betsy and Wheal Friendship (see Chapter Three). Flowing through part of Peter Tavy parish, then into Mary Tavy, it starts from the northern bank of the river at the bottom of the steep slopes of Ger Tor (SX 550830) and for its first ½ mile keeps fairly close to the course of the river itself. At Nat Tor it leaves sight of its parent water-course and turns to run north-westwards for about 1½ miles, then roughly westwards another mile around Willsworthy, and

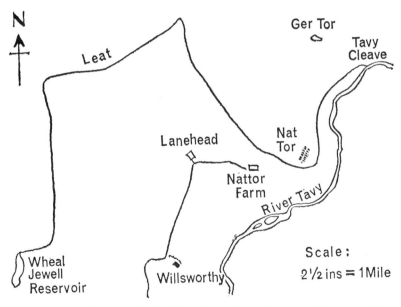

The course of the Reddaford Leat from Tavy Cleave to Wheal Jewell

a similar distance almost due south before turning west again, into Mary Tavy parish, to Wheal Jewell. Here the water, augmented by that brought along the Wheal Jewell leat from the Wallabrook, now enters a reservoir constructed to supply the Mary Tavy Power Station, after which, via the Cholwell Brook, it returns to the Tavy.

The leat, from its point of intake in Tavy Cleave, 1,086 ft above sea level, to Wheal Jewell, 1,060 ft, has a fall of only 26 ft over a distance of $4\frac{1}{2}$ miles—quite a remarkable feat by its constructors who can have had only primitive methods of surveying to assist them. Observation of the leat, especially where it skirts the slopes of Nat Tor, gives the extraordinary impression that the water is running uphill. A further old leat, taking water from the Tavy at Hillbridge (SX 533803) follows a course above the river's right bank, through Kent's Tor cutting to a reservoir from which it is piped to the power station. For ochre works see p. 69.

Mills. The Higher Mill (SX 515776), beside the Colley Brook, now a hay store, contains two millstones and some of the machinery. The wheel is gone. Working ceased around 1914. At Lower Mill (SX 513776), further downstream, though working ceased at the end of the nineteenth century the building stands and here too the grinding stones remain. The waterwheel has long since been removed, though water still runs in the leat, supplying a cattle trough at the nearby farm, and regulated by sluices to prevent flooding.

A waterwheel visible from the road, connected not with the mill but with the farm, has been unused for many years.

Farmhouse. At Cudlipptown are the remains of a sixteenth-century farmhouse (see p. 148).

PLYMPTON
This parish, though outside the area of the National Park, is partially included here on account of its moorland affiliations and because of some interesting mines contained in its northern part. Also Plympton was one of the four stannary towns, being appointed later than the other three, in 1328.

Page 215 (above) *Chair and piece of fish-bellied rail from the Plymouth & Dartmoor Railway, in private garden at Yelverton, 1966;* (below) *The Walkham Viaduct and Gem Mine, photographed about 1887. The wooden cantilevers were replaced by iron around the turn of the century. Demolition of the viaduct was in 1965*

Page 216　(above) *Tollhouse at Moretonhampstead. The list of charges made for use of the turnpike was posted in the recessed panel over the door;* (below) *Moretonhampstead station, 1967*

Mining. In Boringdon Park, near Plym Bridge, are some old shafts and dumps which mark the site of nineteenth-century mining for lead, silver, arsenic and iron. Boringdon Consols' yields for the years 1852–7 included 400 tons of lead ore and 8,000 oz of silver.

For Wheal Sidney (SX 550594), see p. 55; Bottle Hill (SX 564587), see p. 55; Mary Hutchings and Hemerdon Consols (SX 562580 etc), see p. 55; Hemerdon Wolfram Mine (SX 571582), see p. 69.

China-clay working. Only one old chimney remains of the Galva clay drying plant which was situated on the east side of the road ascending Hemerdon Ball, north of Hemerdon village. The clay treated here was obtained from pits at nearby Smallhanger.

Tramway. The route of the Lee Moor Tramway through Cann Wood passed across the north-west corner of the parish.

POSTBRIDGE—see LYDFORD

PRINCETOWN—see LYDFORD

SAMPFORD COURTENAY–STICKLEPATH—see BELSTONE

SAMPFORD SPINEY
Granite working. For quarrying on Pew Tor, see p. 85.

SHAUGH PRIOR
(Although only parts come within the area of the National Park the parish is here treated as a whole)

Early tinning. There is evidence of tinners' workings along the Plym, including the ruins of a mill building on the left (Shaugh) bank above Plym steps where the Plym is joined by the Langcombe Brook. The area drained by the Blacka Brook has also been considerably streamed, while much of the more obvious clay working was on the site of previous tinning.

Mining. Some dumps in Square's Wood (SX 533631), about ½

mile west of the village, on the left bank of the Plym, mark the site of Shaugh Iron Mine. It was active in the years 1870–4 when 4,670 tons were produced.

Granite working. Quarrying for red granite was carried out on Little Trowlesworthy Tor, see p. 85.

China-clay working. For Lee Moor and associated areas, and the Lee Moor Tramway, see pp. 87–95.

The Lee Moor leat brings water to the clayworks from the River Plym, from a point where the river flows between Ditsworthy and Hentor warrens, along a route around Trowlesworthy. This was formerly the leat of Bottle Hill Mine before being adapted in the nineteenth century for clayworking. In order to facilitate the rabbit-drives of Trowlesworthy's warrening days, small footbridges were placed at intervals across it.

Shaugh Bridge clayworks (SX 534636), see p. 91.

Mill. A former corn mill near Shaugh Bridge (SX 532635) has been disused since about 1919. The building and signs of the leat and launder remain.

Field system. The remains of an ancient field system can be seen on the slopes of Hentor Warren, within which lie the ruins of a long-house. Some fields here were still being ploughed by oxen in the eighteenth century.

Warrening. Trowlesworthy Warren lies within the area bounded by the Blacka Brook, the River Plym and Spanish Lake, and includes the two Trowlesworthy Tors. It was the oldest of the known warrens, having been granted by Baldwin de Redvers to Sampson de Traylesworthy some time between 1135 and 1272. In the sixteenth century it was conveyed from John Crocker to William Woollcombe in whose family it has since remained. The warren house is comparatively modern, and replaces an earlier building. The nearby kennel field is surrounded by an 8-ft wall, originally capped by inward projecting stones, with a flight of steps to the top of the wall used at feeding times. Thirty-nine vermin traps have been counted, these being on Great Trowlesworthy Tor and along the banks of the Lee Moor leat.

Willings Walls Warren is a small one, 280 acres, situated between Spanish Lake and the Hentor Brook, the Plym again forming the western boundary. There is no warren house known here, though there are signs of a medieval long-house at the head of Spanish Lake. The warren may have been worked in conjunction with that at Hentor. There are few buries and apparently no vermin traps. Hentor Warren lies between the Hentor and Shavercombe Brooks, and like the other two is bounded by the River Plym to the north-west. At the foot of Hentor are the ruins of the warren house, abandoned probably shortly after the Napoleonic wars. Five vermin traps have been found, as well as buries superimposed on the evidently older field system already mentioned. The warren was worked latterly in conjunction with Ditsworthy, to which it was connected by a wooden bridge across the Plym at the site of the old ford.

SHEEPSTOR

Early tinning. There are considerable remains of tin-working along the valley of the Plym (the right bank of which forms the southeastern border of the parish); also beside the Sheepstor Brook, and beside the Narrator Brook to the north. Remains of tinners' buildings can be seen above the Langcombe confluence on the right bank of the Plym. There are blowing house ruins, and mortar stones on the ground and incorporated in the clapper bridge on the Sheepstor Brook near Colleytown Farm (SX 566674), and remains of another old mine, including a wheelpit and building and also mortar stones near the Narrator Brook in the Deancombe valley (SX 585683). There is another tinners' mill by the Deancombe Brook at Outcombe.

Mining. For Eylesbarrow, see pp. 34 and 45. The small Kit tin mine, south-east of Sheepstor village (SX 563675), was reinvestigated on earlier workings in about 1915. Remains of it are not obvious, shafts on the hill having been filled in, but west of Colleytown a short lane south of the road leads to the remains of buildings connected with it, including a former blacksmith's shop. There are no signs of the stamps photographed here in 1928, but the wheel-pit can be seen, and amongst a clump of trees are to be found three circular buddles.

Warrening. The 230-acre Legis Tor Warren is bounded on the north and west by rabbit-proof walls and on the east by the ruined wall of Ditsworthy; the River Plym forms the boundary along the south side. There are many buries, including the largest known. Also there are eleven vermin traps, including one almost complete; this was damaged in 1967 during a military exercise but an attempt has been made by experts to restore it. There is no evidence of a warren house ever having existed at Legis Tor. Some ironwork of the bridge which connected the two warrens can still be seen below water level just below Spanish Lake.

Ditsworthy Warren, originally of 230 acres, latterly extended from the boundary with Legis Tor Warren up the Plym to Combeshead, Eylesbarrow and Evil Combe, covering 1,100 acres and forming the largest of the warrens. The warren house, abandoned as a dwelling many years ago, is on the southern slopes of Eastern Tor and prob-ably dates from the sixteenth century, with later enlargement. It was served by a leat from Drizzlecombe bringing water right through the house itself. There is a large kennel field, its walls still in fairly good condition, with three dog houses built into them. The many buries were again apparently superimposed on an early field system, and fourteen vermin traps have been recorded, two of them almost com-plete.

Though there is no definite evidence of a warren, three vermin traps have been found on the summit of Sheepstor itself, and five buries on the northern slopes. A ruined house on the lower west face could possibly have been a warren house.

SOURTON

(Only the eastern part of the parish lies within the area; with it is included land common to both Sourton and Bridestowe)

Mining. Torwood Mine (SX 537891), a small copper mine of unknown date, is marked by the remains of old shafts, pronounced tips and general ground disturbance east of Lake Viaduct. The stack of another small copper mine, Sourton Down Consols, or Alice (SX 541915), stands near the junction of the A 30 and A 386 roads near Sourton Cross. The levelled area forms part of Minehouse Farm.

Peat cutting. For the Rattlebrook Peat Railway, see p. 110.

Iceworks. Sourton Tors iceworks, pp. 133–5.

Railway. The now-disused fine nine-arched Lake Viaduct was constructed in the 1870s to carry the London & South Western (later Southern) Railway.

SOUTH BRENT
(Excluding the south-eastern extremity)

Early tinning. Visible evidence of tinning activity includes workings around the source of the Bala Brook.

China-clay working. For Brent Moor clay workings, see p. 95. The remains of clay-treatment plant near Shipley Bridge are also discussed on p. 95.

Peat cutting. The location at Shipley Bridge later used in connection with china clay was earlier a naphtha works (see p. 109).

There are still signs of the Zeal Tor Tramway which can be found by ascending the hillside, crossing the road leading to the water-treatment works and continuing just above the works and the wall alongside until the end of the wall is reached. There is a slight cutting above the wall, and shortly afterwards the track, now grassy, can be fairly clearly determined, and a number of the metal bolts which secured the wooden rails to granite blocks can be seen at approximately 9-ft intervals. The tramway connected the naphtha works with the peat ties at Redlake, and the eastern section was used later by the clay company (p. 95).

Mills. At SX 695608, above Lydia Bridge, on the west bank of the Avon, in the grounds of a private house, are some fairly massive remains of buildings in which sail-cloth was produced, probably until the 1870s. Lydia Mill was owned by the family of William Crossing, the Dartmoor writer, and he worked there for a time in his younger days. The large iron wheel is still in position. On the outside of one of the walls surrounding it is a small subsidiary wheel which, activated by the main wheel, was last used earlier in the present century to work crushing machinery in a quarry on the opposite side of the river. Water still flows in the leat from the weir on the Avon just above. Above the wheel-pit is the shell of a very substantial stone building which was probably used as a store for raw materials or finished products. Another three-storey building formerly stood on the site of the present garden lawn.

On the south side of the bridge, on the same side of the river, is a former wheelwright's shop, now converted to a dwelling house. The incomplete waterwheel is still in position.

At Brent Mill (SX 697596), formerly the manor mills—grist mills that later became flock mills utilising rags—some old buildings remain amid newer premises in which wooden bedding frames are manufactured.

SOUTH TAWTON
(Southern part only)

Mining. There are practically no visible remains of the small Gooseford tin mine, south of the hamlet of Gooseford (SX 676918). It was worked over for arsenic in the earlier years of the present century. Ivy Tor Mine is marked by some slight open cuttings on the south side of the River Taw (SX 627935). Latterly it was worked in conjunction with the Belstone mines until 1892. Ford Mine (SX 643935) is marked by the remains of a shaft and dumps just across the field from Ford Farm, to the south-west. Copper and arsenic were obtained here early in the present century. For Ramsley (SX 650930), see p. 62.

Mills. There are no spectacular remains of any of the mills which once flourished in the parish, served by the leat from the Blackaton Brook. The ancient Frog Mill, just below the intake of the leat, near the Throwleigh border, is reduced to ruined stone walls.

Warrening. Fifteen buries found on the slopes of the hillside south-west of the Taw are probably the remains of Skaigh Warren, a comparatively modern warren. No warren house is known, and no vermin traps.

SOUTH ZEAL—see SOUTH TAWTON

STICKLEPATH—see BELSTONE

TAVISTOCK

The parish is only fractionally within the area of the National Park and is included as a whole in *The Industrial Archaeology of the Tamar Valley* by Frank Booker. Just the eastern fringes are included here.

Early tinning. Tavistock was one of the four stannary towns, appointed in 1305.

Mining. West Friendship Mine, near Brinsabatch (SX 485796) was worked for copper in the 1850s and '60s. A few overgrown tips remain.

Mill. Taviton Mill (SX 500744) has over centuries been a mill for tanning, wool, and corn. Now a residence.

THROWLEIGH

Early tinning. There is some evidence of tinning excavations on the western slopes of Kennon Hill.

Granite working. A certain amount of granite 'ripping' was done on the west side of Kennon, being continued at times in the 1930s.

Farming. Higher Shilstone (SX 660901) is a fine example of a granite built thatched Dartmoor longhouse dating from the 16th–17th centuries, with the passage between the dwelling and shippon still surviving.

UGBOROUGH

(The narrowing northern strip of the parish extends into the Dartmoor area)

Early tinning. There are remains of tinners' workings in the vicinity of the East and West Glaze Brooks, and the remains of a tinners' mill and of another tinners' building on the west bank below Glazemeet.

Granite working. Disused granite quarry on the slopes of Western Beacon, see p. 85.

China-clay working. The disused Redlake Mineral Railway track starts at Bittaford and runs northwards over Ugborough Moor for the greater part of its way (see p. 96).

Mill. Owley Mill (SX 676599), which was for corn, lost its water-wheel long ago. It is suggested that the name here is from the 'owlers' who led their pack animals across the small bridge over the Glaze Brook on the old route via Spurrell's Cross.

WALKHAMPTON

Early tinning. There is evidence of tinners' workings on the east side of the Walkham above Merrivale, including the ruins of two blowing houses (see p. 32), and along the Meavy with tinners' mills including two at Black Tor Falls (p. 32). At Norsworthy (SX 567696) there are tin mill remains on the Meavy's left bank with several mortar stones, and opposite, on the right bank, the remains of another tinners' mill with wheelpit and leat.

There are also open gullies left by tinners, and other remains of working at Riddipit, Keaglesborough, Crazy Well Pool and points farther east.

Mining. The small Wheal George and Huckworthy Bridge copper mines (SX 529704 and 533706), the former below and the latter above Huckworthy Bridge, operated in the 1850s. Wheal George is marked by some fairly large mounds, mostly of loose rubble, and some filled shafts. Huckworthy Bridge Mine site is marked by mounds and shaft remains. Walkhampton Consols (SX 522697), also known as Wheal Rose, was another small copper mine. Signs of it still remain in a narrow field near the river to the north of the Horrabridge–Walkhampton road just as it enters Knowle Down.

Furzehill Mine, though a large number of its shafts are in Furzehill Wood and thus in Walkhampton parish, is described under Horrabridge (p. 199). (Horrabridge only became a civil parish in 1951 so that previously the whole of the mine, including the later workings, was in Walkhampton.) The site is dangerous.

Granite working. King Tor, Swell Tor and Foggintor Quarries, see pp. 81–3.

Mills. The building of Huckworthy Mill (SX 532705), recently modernized, stands on the east side of the river above the bridge. The wheel is gone and the wheel-pit filled in.

The name 'Mill' in the village is a misnomer. The overshot cast iron waterwheel still in position served a wheelwright's shop established in 1845. Business declined latterly and the premises became used for other trades, but it is hoped the craft may be revived and sustained for modern demands—wheels for carriages and military and museum requirements etc.

Farming. Potato cave near the abandoned Leather Tor Farm (SX 567698), see pp. 150–1.

Warrening. There are ten small buries near the road (A384) east of Merrivale within a walled area extending to the slopes of Great Mis Tor, bounded on the west by the River Walkham. Merrivale Warren probably dates from around 1800 and was short-lived. It is said to have been made by a Mr Watts, who also built the cottage, of which a few stone remains can be seen beside the road near Over Tor. Fourteen small buries have been noted between the road and Over Tor, of a similar type to those in the enclosure.

Railway. The route of the Princetown Railway, mainly coincident here with that of the earlier Plymouth & Dartmoor, can be followed winding and ascending over Walkhampton Common (see Chapter Nine).

WHITCHURCH

Mining. Merrivale Bridge Mine, or Wheal Fortune (SX 552753) was a minor nineteenth century working for tin; a wheelpit, leats and pits are traceable. Beckamoor Combe, extending above and below the

Tavistock–Princetown road (B 3357) at the top of Pork Hill is a large open working streamed for tin as late as 1860. A small building, probably a miners' shelter, remains at the upper end (SX 535757). Devon Burra Burra Mine, or Wheal Gatepost (SX 514741), marked by overgrown tips and workings south of Moorshop Cross, and Wheal Surprise (SX 514740), south of the stream westwards from Pennycomequick, were nineteenth century copper workings. Great Sortridge and other small 'Sortridge' mines (different from Sortridge Great Consols, see HORRABRIDGE) on Plaster Down (east and west from SX 514724) were mainly trial works of around the 1850s; prominent mounds remain but a chimney has long since gone. Furzeland Down Mine (SX 496707) has left shallow pits and overgrown workings, while on the opposite side of the Tavistock–Plymouth road (A 386) on the east bank of the Walkham are the remains of Gem Mine or West Sortridge Consols (SX 494706), a tin mine worked from the 1850s to '70s. Shafts were filled with stone from the Walkham railway viaduct which crossed the valley here, after demolition in 1965; Gem Cottage was the former count house. A line of pits on West Down are the result of past prospecting for Sortridge and Bedford Mines. Devon & Courtenay Consols (SX 474717) is marked by a large mound, shafts farther west in Birch Woods have been levelled by the Forestry Commission. For Rixhill and Anderton see p. 56.

Granite working. For granite working on Pew Tor and Staple Tor, including sett-making and Merrivale Quarry, see pp. 74–6.

Heckwood Quarry (SX 545738), see p. 84.

Water supply. Grimstone and Sortridge leat, see p. 139.

Railway. The disused line of the former South Devon & Tavistock (later Great Western) Railway runs through the parish, with a tunnel beneath the Halfway House at Grenofen.

WIDECOMBE-IN-THE-MOOR

Early tinning. There is evidence of early tinning activity, parti-

cularly in the valley of the West Webburn. A tin-streaming pond
was at SX 711785, see p. 25.

Mills. Jordan Mill (SX 700750), a one-time corn mill on the West
Webburn, probably dates from the fifteenth century and was last
used in the early 1920s. It is now charmingly converted to a dwelling-
house. Some old grinding-stones are incorporated in the crazy paving
in the garden and an old wooden wheel axle with iron straps is in use
as a gatepost by the bridge over the stream. The leat is traceable upstream. Also on the West Webburn, Ponsworthy Mill (SX 701738) is
now a holiday cottage. There are the remains of a waterwheel. A
nineteenth century sketch by Frederick Foot in the Torquay Natural
History Museum shows the mill with two waterwheels in line.
Ponsworthy was formerly a busy place with several workshops: a
bakehouse, wheelwright's shop with forge, another forge, a shoe
maker and a tailor.

Cockingford Mill (SX 717751), on the East Webburn, is now a
farm, and a guest house in the summer. The somewhat derelict wheel
at the end of the building can be seen from the road.

Agriculture. There is evidence of early agricultural systems in this
parish, notably in the vicinity of Blackaton (see p. 146) and at the
northern end of Corndon Down.

Warrening. Vaghill Warren, of about 520 acres, dates from 1613,
though its life was probably short. It is bounded by the River Dart on
the south and west, by Yar Tor on the north, Corndon Tor on the
north-east and Lug Tor on the south-east. Ruined buildings in
Eastern Combe may be associated with a warren house. Two buries
have been found adjacent to its field walls, others on the western
slopes of Eastern Combe and the southern slopes of Vaghill as far as
Lug Tor, totalling twenty-five in all. There are the remains of three
vermin traps, two of them against prehistoric field walls.

YELVERTON—see BUCKLAND MONACHORUM

Bibliography

GENERAL

Crossing, William, *Guide to Dartmoor* (1912, repub. 1965). Reprinted Peninsula Press 1990
Crossing, William, *Hundred Years on Dartmoor* (1901, repub. 1967)
Crossing, William, *Dartmoor Worker* (1903 articles ed. B. Le Messurier 1966). Reprinted Peninsula Press 1992
Devon Archaeology Society. *Devon Archaeology 3* (Various articles)
Gill, Crispin, ed. *Dartmoor: A New Study* (David & Charles, 1970)
Hemery, Eric. *High Dartmoor* (Hale, 1983)
Hemery, Eric. *Walking the Dartmoor Railroads* (1983). Reprinted Peninsula Press 1991
Hemery, Eric. *Walking the Dartmoor Waterways* (1986). Reprinted Peninsula Press 1991
Hoskins, W. G. *Devon* (Collins, 1954)
Le Messurier, Brian. 'The post-prehistoric structures of central north Dartmoor' *Trans Devonshire Association* 111 (1979)
Perkins, John W. *Geology Explained: Dartmoor and the Tamar Valley* (David & Charles, 1974)
Robins, John. *Follow the Leat* (Enlarged edition 1984)
Somers Cocks, John, and Greeves, Tom. *A Dartmoor Century 1883–1983 (Dartmoor Preservation Association,* 1983)
Worth, R. Hansford. *Dartmoor* (1953, repub. 1967)

EARLY TINNING AND LATER MINING

Atkinson, M. and Schmitz, C. 'Kelly Iron Mine, near Bovey Tracey' *Devon Historian* 11 (October 1975)
Atkinson, M., Burt, R., and Waite, P. *Dartmoor Mines: the mines of the granite mass* (University of Exeter, 1978)
Beer, K. E. 'Mineralisation in the Teign Valley' *Trans Devonshire Association* 110 (1978)
Brewer, Dave. 'Ringleshutes Tin Mine' *Dartmoor Magazine* 11 (Summer 1988)
Broughton, D. G. 'Tin working in the eastern district of the parish of Chagford, Devon' *Proc. Geologists' Assoc.* 78. 3. (1967)
Broughton, D. G. 'Dartmoor Tin Working: its effect upon scenery and landscape' *Kingston Geographer* (1968)
Broughton, D. G. 'The Birch Tor and Vitifer mining complex' *Trans Cornish Institute of Engineers* 24 (1968–9)
Burt, R., Waite, P., and Burnley, R., *Devon and Somerset Mines: metalliferous and associated minerals 1845–1913* (University of Exeter 1984)
Collins, J. H. *Observations on the West of England Mining Region* (1912)
Cook, R. M. L., Greeves, T. A. P., and Kilvington, C. C. 'Eylesbarrow (1814–1852): a study of a Dartmoor tin mine' *Trans Devonshire Association* 106 (1974)
Costello, L. M. 'The Bradford Pool Case' *Trans Devonshire Association* 113 (1981)
Dines, H. G. *Metalliferous Mining Region of South-West England Vol II* (1956)
Finberg, H. P. R. *Tavistock Abbey* (1951)

French, H. and Linehan, C. D. appendix to 'Abandoned Medieval sites in Widecombe-in-the-Moor' *Trans Devonshire Association* 95 (1963)

Greeves, T. A. P. 'A mine in the Deancombe Valley' *Trans Devonshire Association* 101 (1969)

Greeves, T. A. P. 'A tinners' mill in Walkhampton parish' *Trans Devonshire Association* 103 (1971)

Greeves, T. A. P. 'Wheal Prosper, a little known Dartmoor tin mine' *Plymouth Mineral and Mining Club Journal* 6 (1975)

Greeves, T. A. P. 'Merrivale Bridge Mine, Wheal Fortune and Staple Tor sett 1806–1887' *Plymouth Mineral and Mining Club Journal* 6:3 (1976)

Greeves, T. A. P. 'Wheal Cumpston Tin Mine, Holne, Devon' *Trans Devonshire Association* 110 (1978)

Greeves, T. A. P. 'History of Whiteworks Tin Mine Part 1. 1790–1848' *Plymouth Mineral and Mining Club Journal* 11:2 (1980)

Greeves, T. A. P. *The Devon Tin Industry* 1450–1750: an Archaeological and Historical Survey 1981 Unpub. Ph.D. Thesis. University of Exeter.

Greeves, T. A. P. 'The archaeological potential of the Devon tin industry' *Medieval Industry* (Crossley ed. 1981) (Council for British Archaeology research report, 40)

Greeves, T. A. P. 'Steeperton Tor tin mine, Dartmoor, Devon' *Trans Devonshire Association* 117 (1985)

Greeves, Tom. *Tin Mines and Miners of Dartmoor: a photographic record* (Devon Books, 1986)

Greeves, T. A. P. 'The Great Courts or Parliaments of Devon Tinners 1474–1796' *Trans Devonshire Association* 119 (1987)

Greeves, T. A. P. 'Blowing & Knocking—The Dartmoor Tin Mills before 1750' *Dartmoor Magazine* 23 (Summer 1991)

Hamilton Jenkin, A. K. *Mines of Devon Vol 1*: the southern area (David & Charles, 1974)

Hamilton Jenkin, A. K. 'Mines of Devon, north and east of Dartmoor' (Devon Library Services 1981)

Harris, Helen. 'A Dartmoor Ochre Works' *Devon Historian* 43 (October 1991)

Lewis, G. R. *The Stannaries* (1908, repub. 1965)

Newman, P. 'The Moorland Meavy—a Tinners' Landscape' *Trans Devonshire Association* 119 (1987)

Newman, P. 'Two small mines in the Newleycombe Valley' *Dartmoor Magazine* 8 (Autumn 1987)

Newman, P. 'The Tin Mill at Riddipit' *Dartmoor Magazine* 12 (Autumn 1988)

Newman, P. 'One Hundred Years at Black Tor Falls' Part 1 in *Dartmoor Magazine* 21 (Winter 1990), Part 2 in *Dartmoor Magazine* 22 (Spring 1991)

Rendell, Paul. 'Bottle Hill Mine' *Plymouth Mineral and Mining Club Journal* 20, 3

Richardson, P. H. G. 'Hexworthy Tin Mine' *Plymouth Mineral and Mining Club Journal* 3:3 and 4:2 (1973)

Richardson, P. H. G. 'Roborough Down Wolfram' *Plymouth Mineral and Mining Club Journal* 17, 1 (December 1986)

Richardson, P. H. G. 'Last years at Golden Dagger Mine' *Dartmoor Magazine* 17 (Winter 1989)

Roberts, S. and Richardson, P. H. G. 'Iron Mining at Shaugh Prior'. *Plymouth Mineral and Mining Club Journal* 19, 1 (May 1989)

Schmitz, C. J. 'The early growth of the Devon barytes industry, 1835–1875' *Trans Devonshire Association* 106 (1974)
Schmitz, C. J. 'The Development and decline of the Devon barytes industry, 1875–1958' *Trans Devonshire Association* 109 (1977)
Schmitz, C. J. 'The Teign Valley lead mines' *Northern Cavern and Mine Research Society occasional publications* 6

INDUSTRIES FROM GRANITE

Allen, A. J. 'Dewerstone Trackways' *Western Morning News* 5 Nov 1962
Barton, R. M. *History of the China Clay Industry* (1966)
Brewer, Kath. 'The Foggintor Area—Part 1' *Dartmoor Magazine* 6 (Spring 1987); 'The Foggintor Area—Part 2' *Dartmoor Magazine* 7 (Summer 1987); 'The Foggintor Cottages' *Dartmoor Magazine* 23 (Summer 1991)
Ewens, M. C. *The Haytor Granite Tramway and Stover Canal* (David & Charles, 1977)
Hall, R. M. S. *The Lee Moor Tramway* (Oakwood Press)
Harris, Helen. 'Nineteenth Century granite working on Pew Tor and Staple Tor, western Dartmoor' *Trans Devonshire Association* 113 (1981)
Meade-King, W. O. 'Lee Moor Railway' *ECC Review* (Autumn 1961)
Rendell, Paul. 'China Clay on Walkhampton Common' *Dartmoor Magazine* 20 (Autumn 1990)
Robinson, Rosemary. 'The early china clay industry on Brent Moor' *Plymouth Mineral and Mining Club Journal* 11:1
Somers Cocks, J. 'The Haytor Granite Quarries' *Devon and Cornwall Notes and Queries* 32
Wade, E. A. *The Redlake Tramway and China Clay Works* (Twelveheads Press 1982)

PEAT

Crossing, William. 'Echoes of an ancient forest' 10 and 11 *Western Morning News* series 1901
Woolner, Diana *Devon and Cornwall Notes and Queries* 30:4 (October 1965)

MILLS AND MISCELLANEOUS

Barron, R. A. *The Finch Foundry Trust and Sticklepath Museum of Rural Industry*
Gill, Crispin. *Plymouth, a New History* (David & Charles 1966)
Harris, Helen. 'The Sourton Tors Iceworks, North-west Dartmoor, 1874–86' *Trans Devonshire Association* 120 (1988)
Hellier, J. 'The pioneers who gave Devon the lead in hydro-electricity power' *Western Morning News* 18 February 1967
Pye, A. R. and Robinson, R. *An Archaeological Survey of the Gunpowder Factory at Powdermills Farm, Postbridge, Devon* (Exeter Museums Archaeological Field Unit 1990)
Shorter, A. H. 'The historical geography of the paper-making industry in Devon 1684–1950' *Trans Devonshire Association* 82 (1950)
Stanbrook, Elisabeth. 'Fingle Mill' *Dartmoor Magazine* 21 (Winter 1990)

AGRICULTURE AND KINDRED PURSUITS

Beresford, Guy. 'Three Medieval settlements on Dartmoor' A report on the late E. Marie Minter's excavations. *Medieval Archaeology XXIII* (1979)

Fleming, Andrew. 'The Prehistoric landscape of Dartmoor, Part 1, South Dartmoor' *Proceedings of the Prehistoric Society* (1978)

Fleming, Andrew. 'The Prehistoric landscape of Dartmoor, Part 2, North and East Dartmoor' *Proceedings of the Prehistoric Society* (1983)

Fleming, Andrew. *The Dartmoor Reaves* Batsford 1988

French, H. and Linehan, C. D. 'Abandoned Medieval sites in Widecombe-in-the-Moor' *Trans Devonshire Association* 95 (1963)

Gawne, E. and Somers Cocks, J. 'Parallel reaves on Dartmoor' *Trans Devonshire Association* 100 (1968)

Haynes, R. G. 'Vermin Traps and Rabbit Warrens on Dartmoor' *Post Medieval Archaeology IV* (1970)

Hoskins, R. G. *Old Devon* (David & Charles, 1966)

Linehan, C. D. 'Deserted sites of Dartmoor' *Trans Devonshire Association* 97 (1965)

Millward, Roy, and Robinson, Adrian. *Dartmoor and South Devon* (Macmillan, 1971)

COMMUNICATIONS

Kendall, H. G. *The Plymouth and Dartmoor Railway* (Oakwood Press, 1968)

Le Messurier, Brian. 'The Philpotts peat passes of northern Dartmoor: a pioneer survey' *Trans Devonshire Association* 97 (1965)

Thomas, David St John. *Regional Railway History Vol 1 – The West Country* (third edition) (David & Charles, 1966)

PARISHES

Govier, L. *Walkhampton Church, Parish and Village* (1984)

A History of Holne (Holne Parish Council, 1977)

The Village of Horrabridge

Acknowledgments

THE kind and willing help of very many people has made it possible for me to write this book.

My foremost thanks must go to Mr John Somers Cocks. His initial encouragement helped me embark on the project, and the readiness with which he made available his store of Dartmoor knowledge greatly eased the way. Later, he kindly read my manuscript, giving criticism and advice, and he provided the sectional drawing of Silverbrook Mine (p. 67), and a pre-drawing for my sketch of 'feather and tare' (p. 74). I am also deeply grateful to Mr Brian Le Messurier; at the outset he generously volunteered any help he could give and throughout has provided me with considerable information, particularly with regard to site details on the moor.

A number of people have been very helpful in giving first-hand local information to aid my investigations in their particular parishes, and I would specially thank: Mr and Mrs E. Alford; Miss J. Bellamy; Captain H. P. Chichester Clark; Mrs M. Coaker; Mr E. Conybeare; Mr R. M. Elliott; Mr R. Gallup; Mr L. Govier; Mrs M. Mudge; Mr W. Perryman; Brigadier A. H. Peskett; Mr G. B. Preston; Mrs M. Pyne; Mr J. Ray; Miss A. Staplin; Mr R. L. Taverner; the late Brigadier G. Welchman; Mrs M. Windeat; and Mrs E. B. Wonnacott.

I am most grateful to the numerous owners and occupiers who have allowed me to inspect industrial remains on their land, and who have provided information.

On the subject of mining I am much indebted to Mr Hermon French for his kindly elucidation of the geological and technical aspects of Dartmoor mining, as well as for the pre-drawing of the sketch of a longitudinal section of a Dartmoor tin mine (p. 42). Mr R. A. Gorges, Principal of the Camborne School of Metalliferous

Mining, has also provided information on mining techniques. Mr W. Joint has been generous in passing on knowledge he has gained from personal explorations of old workings. Surgeon-Captain R. G. Anthony has given me information of site details of certain tinning and mining remains, and Mr Frank Booker has been helpful over various mining problems. All these I thank, as well as the following, who most kindly assisted by talking of their own personal experiences of Dartmoor mining days: Mr and Mrs J. Bellamy; Mrs Cooper; the late Mr H. Leaman; Mr C. Rowland and Mr W. G. Stephens.

For information about past granite working on the western side of the moor I gratefully thank Mr J. C. Rooke, and also Mr R. J. Tall of English Clays Lovering Pochin & Co Ltd, who enlightened me by his knowledge of Lee Moor past and present, Miss Rosalind Cooke who generously allowed me to see her thesis on china clay, and Mr W. Trust for telling me of his experiences as a clay-worker at Redlake.

The late Mr Walter Alford was of immense help with first-hand details about working conditions at the Rattlebrook Peatworks.

For historical and other information on various mills still in industrial use I must thank: Mr W. G. Chaffe and others of the CWS woollen mill, Buckfastleigh; Mr Edworthy of the Buckfast Spinning Company; Mr Layzell of the Buckfast Plating Company; Messrs A. Morris & Sons (Dunsford) Ltd and Miss E. M. Ridge of Messrs Portals (John Allen & Sons) Ltd. Mr R. G. Stephens helped considerably in my original investigation of the Powder Mills, and Mr P. J. Stuckey, Plymouth City Water Engineer, and Mr S. Jackman, of the Central Electricity Generating Board, Mary Tavy, provided details about the leats under their respective responsibilities.

In agricultural matters Mr Peter Holmes, County Agricultural Adviser, Ministry of Agriculture, has been most helpful; Mr R. G. Haynes has generously lent me the extensive notes of his own research on the subject of warrening with his sketches of vermin traps which I have copied (p. 157); Mr. J. Stevenson provided information about fur farming.

Mr Roger Sellick kindly answered queries about the Plymouth &

Dartmoor Railway. Mrs Janet Shorrock also deserves sincere thanks for certain site investigations she willingly undertook on my behalf. And I would also express gratitude for information given by Mr H. A. Bowditch, National Parks Divisional Planning Officer; and Mr S. G. Jenkins, Clerk to Tavistock Rural District Council. The Map Room staff of the British Museum have been most helpful, and the staff of the Derbyshire County Library have gone to great lengths in obtaining books for me.

Sincere thanks are given to those people who have kindly lent me photographs, and I am grateful for the special care taken by Messrs Jon Wooldridge Ltd in the developing and printing of my photographic material.

Thanks are also due to the Editor of *The Western Morning News* for allowing me to reproduce articles and photographs of mine originally published in that paper, my publishers for suggesting the writing of the book and for their helpful attention during my work on it, and to Mr Crispin Gill for further criticism and advice over the manuscript.

Members of my family and friends have in various ways made it possible for me to get on with the work; and I thank my children for their co-operation and for their forebearance with a mother seemingly perpetually surrounded by maps, papers and an obsession for Dartmoor. Finally I thank my husband; his sharper eyes have often been the ones to spot obscure site details on our moorland walks, and I could not have written the book without the tremendous encouragement and support he has given me.

Helen Harris
1968

For the revision I have been glad to consult again my friends Mr John Somers Cocks and Mr Brian Le Messurier, and also Dr Tom Greeves, whose recent extended works have so considerably added to Dartmoor mining knowledge. I am grateful, too, to owners and occupiers of sites who have kindly allowed access, and to firms and their representatives, and others, for information. My thanks to them all.

Helen Harris
1986

Index